Praise for Conversations Kids at Every Age and Stage

"I am a strong believer in the Money Personality philosophies of Scott and Bethany Palmer. This book focuses on children, but in reality applies to many relationships. I have read their other books, and they have shown me how to strengthen my relationships by understanding the five Money Personalities within each of us. These five money conversations are universal and work with adults, parents, coworkers, and friends."

— Bob and Susan Meeder
President/CEO and
chief operations officer
Meeder Investment
Management

"What can I say? I love this book! It's the aha moment that so many parents need today! When you understand not only your own Money Personality but your children's, too, you'll be far better equipped to train them in the way they should go, the way God has wired them to be for his purposes. Scott and Bethany have written a handbook that will help you navigate money conversations with your kids: from entitlement to responsibility, from allowances to special activities, from impulse purchases to saving for the future. If you're a parent, you'll want to read this book."

— Susie Larson
Radio host, national speaker,
author of *Your Beautiful
Purpose*

THE M**5**NEY
Conversations
to Have with Your Kids
at Every Age and Stage

Scott & Bethany Palmer
THE MONEY COUPLE®

W PUBLISHING GROUP

AN IMPRINT OF THOMAS NELSON

Published in Nashville, Tennessee, by W Publishing Group, an imprint of Thomas Nelson.

Thomas Nelson titles may be purchased in bulk for educational, business, fund-raising, or sales promotional use. For information, e-mail SpecialMarkets@ ThomasNelson.com.

Library of Congress Cataloging-in-Publication Data

Palmer, Scott, 1971–
  The 5 money conversations to have with your kids at every age and stage / Scott Palmer and Bethany Palmer.
    pages cm
  ISBN 978-0-8499-6479-4 (paperback)
1. Children—Finance, Personal. 2. Teenagers—Finance, Personal. I. Palmer, Bethany, 1965– II. Title. III. Title: Five money conversations to have with your kids at every age and stage.
  HG179.P18868 2014
  332.024—dc23   2014020186

Printed in the United States of America

14 15 16 17 18 19 RRD 6 5 4 3 2 1

*We dedicate this book to our kids,
Cole and Cade.*

*Thank you for what you are teaching us
about your Money Personalities and how
God has created you both so uniquely.
We love you both!*

Contents

Section 3: Ages 13–17

Section 4: Ages 18 and Beyond

Acknowledgments

We are so thankful for the amazing people God has put in our lives. Thank you to all the amazing couples we have worked with over the past year. Thank you for opening up your lives and the lives of your kids to us.

Thank you to Matt Baugher and the amazing team in the W Publishing Group at Thomas Nelson. Thank you for believing in our message and our passion to make families better.

Carla Barnhill continues to be such a great support for us and has helped us shape our message for our readers.

Thank you to our amazing church in Colorado Springs, New Life Church. Pastor Brady Boyd and Pastor Garvin McCarrell are such a huge blessing and support to us.

Our goal is to change families for the better—to help them understand how they can have amazing Money Relationships and strong family ties.

SECTION 1

. . .

Your Money Relationship

1

Money and Relationships

Raise your hand if your parents had "the talk" with you. No, not *that* talk. We mean the talk about how to balance a checkbook and manage your savings and plan for the future. Our guess is that there aren't many hands in the air.

Those of us who grew up in the 1970s and 80s were as likely to have money conversations with our parents as we were conversations about the birds and the bees. For our parents, the idea that you would intentionally teach your kids about money wasn't really on the radar. Their parents—our Depression-era grandparents—didn't talk about money, so ours didn't either.

Add to that, most of us came of age in a time when the economic future looked pretty bright. Until recently, every generation has experienced more prosperity than the generation before it. But that's changing. There are conflicting predictions about what the future might be like for our kids, but one thing is for sure—our kids are going to need some money smarts to navigate their futures.

We meet with thousands of couples every year to help them sort out their finances. And in the past ten years, we've discovered that the skills people need to figure out their money issues have almost nothing to do with crunching numbers or understanding global markets. Instead, we've found that what couples really need to manage their money is strong communication, the ability to understand each other, and a commitment to putting their relationship above their budget.

The same is true when it comes to helping your kids learn about money. We hear from parents all the time:

"My son is so irresponsible with money."

"My child spends her allowance on the most useless stuff."

"I'm sick of my kids begging for toys every time we go to the store."

"Our kids expect us to spend a fortune on them at Christmas."

"Our son needs to start saving money to help pay for college, but he can't seem to do it."

Parents talk to us about these issues because they want their kids to avoid the money conflicts and anxieties and mistakes they've dealt with. They worry that if they don't give their kids money management skills now, their kids will bounce checks and run up credit card debt and never have a dime in a savings account. And for the most part, they're right.

Our kids need us to teach them about money. The skills

we need to manage our finances don't come naturally for most of us. So it's essential that of the many life skills we pass on to our kids, money management is close to the top of the list. But there's another set of money-related skills that most parents never think about, because most of us don't have those skills ourselves.

Every money problem, every money fight, every money conversation has two layers. The first layer involves the financial details—your budget, your savings account, your debt and retirement and college funds and phone bills and parking tickets, and so on. Those are your finances, and that's all important stuff.

But it's the second, more foundational layer that we want to uncover in this book. We think of it as your Money Relationship—the how and why underneath those financial details. It's those deep-seated assumptions and beliefs you bring to the decisions you make that involve money. And every decision you make as a family involves money.

Really. Think about it for a minute. The kind of house you live in? A money decision. The kind of jobs you have? A money decision. The cars you drive, the shoes you wear, the coffee you drink, the TV shows you get? All money decisions.

And when kids are involved, the money component of those daily decisions becomes even clearer. Hospital birth or home birth? Work or stay home? Cloth or disposable? Homemade baby food or store bought? Public school or private school? New clothes or hand-me-downs? Allowances, birthday presents, checkout-line goodies, another field trip fee, more new shoes, summer camp, piano lessons, broken backpacks, this winter's growth spurt, and on and on it goes.

Every year the US Department of Agriculture puts together a report, "Expenditures on Children by Families." The 2013 report, which includes everything from housing and food to health care and school expenses, puts the average yearly cost of raising a child around $13,000 to $15,000. Per child. Per year. Good grief!

All those money decisions mean that families are thinking about and dealing with money at least once a day if not more. And not just the details of these decisions but the emotions and expectations behind them. Your preschooler wants a quarter for a gumball at the coffee shop. Your teenager needs a check for $80 to pay her booster fee for the tennis team. Your sixth grader wants to use his allowance to buy a new game for his DS. None of these decisions will break your budget, but all of them have implications for your relationship with your child.

When your preschooler asks for a gumball, you're not thinking about the quarter. You're thinking about how many times your child asks for something and whether you'll create a greedy little monster if you always say yes. The check for the tennis team isn't just a booster fee. It's also a sign that you support your child's interests, or it's a moment to hand over some financial responsibility to her, or it may be a time to talk about just how packed her schedule may become. And that DS game isn't just a game. It's a chance to show your child that you trust his judgment, or a time to put the kibosh on a habit that has gotten out of hand, or an opportunity to teach some great lessons about delayed gratification.

Every one of these seemingly straightforward money

decisions is the tip of the Money Relationship iceberg. If you know how to navigate your way through the relationship side of these decisions, you'll find that you not only help your kids make smart money decisions but also strengthen your mutual emotional bonds. Misread the signs and you risk a breach in the keel that keeps a family close and connected.

When Bethany was a teenager, she was a nationally ranked competitive swimmer. Her coach wanted her to attend a big-deal training camp with an Olympic training team. It was a huge opportunity for Bethany, and she was honored to be invited to the camp. As Bethany was preparing for the trip, her coach called to let Bethany's mom know they had to buy a special team swimsuit for the camp. Bethany's mom, who hates to spend money, thought that was ridiculous. In her mind, Bethany had enough swimsuits already and certainly didn't need another one that would cost $35. Bethany heard her mom's conversation with the coach and her mom's refusal to buy the suit. And she was crushed.

For Bethany's mom, this was a financial decision. But for Bethany, her mom's unwillingness to buy the suit felt like a lack of support for her dreams. In Bethany's mind, this camp was a once-in-a-lifetime opportunity, and now her mom couldn't spend $35 on it? Wasn't she worth that much?

The sting of that decision hurt and created real emotional distance between Bethany and her mom. Obviously Bethany's mom didn't mean to hurt her daughter. And now as an adult, Bethany understands the way her mom thinks about money.

When we get parents talking about their own childhood

experiences with earning an allowance or going on vacation or getting their first jobs, they always have a story like Bethany's, a time when a financial decision became a point of contention between them and their parents.

Henry told us how he planned on saving his paper route money so he could buy a new bike, only to find out that his parents expected him to use his income to buy his own clothes and school supplies.

Peter remembered having a huge blowup with his father when he bought his first car. His dad insisted that he buy something economical and safe, while Peter was determined to buy a cool set of wheels he could customize.

Rachelle's mom was as thrifty as they get, and she rarely bought new clothes and toys for her children. Even when Rachelle begged her parents for a new toy at Christmas, every Christmas morning brought the same kind of second-hand dolls and used clothes she had come to expect. "If we had been really poor, I would have understood," said Rachelle, "but we had money. My mom just didn't like to spend money on things that she knew we'd outgrow or break. I suppose she was trying to be smart with her spending, but I just saw it as her caring more about saving money than giving her kids something special."

You probably have a few stories like this too. Most of us can think of a time when we butted heads with our parents over a money decision. And if you still remember it, it's because you had an emotional response to that conflict, a response that created tension between you and your parents. You can butt heads at age seven or seventy; the reality is . . . it will happen.

That's the Money Relationship at work.

Your Money Relationship has nothing to do with how much you spend on your kids. It has nothing to do with how much you've saved for college or how much allowance you give. It has nothing to do with how much debt you have or how much you've invested. Those are your financial arrangements, and we're not going to spend much time discussing those here.

Instead, we're going to dig into what really makes or breaks a family—your relationships. You can have a great budget, a healthy college fund, and a great system for doling out allowances, but if you are constantly bickering with your kids about their spending, missing out on making memories now in order to fund their futures, or putting all your energies into making sure every child is earning every cent of his or her allowance, well, you've hit the wrong target. You might have a solid financial future, but you'll have a family that can barely be in a room together without fighting.

That's why we're going to focus on the Money Relationship between you and your kids. All the chore charts and savings plans in the world aren't worth a thing if you have broken relationships. As we focus on your Money Relationship, you'll notice that we refer to your *parenting partner* instead of your *spouse*. We've been intentional about that language as a way of acknowledging that a family isn't always two married people and their children. We want to make sure single parents and blended families with moms, dads, and stepparents feel encouraged to take on these conversations as well. It's essential that all of the primary adults in your children's lives are working together to help build these money skills.

We're going to use the next two chapters to lay the foundation for building a strong, healthy Money Relationship with your kids. Then we'll kick into high gear and work through the biggest challenges parents face when helping their kids learn how to think about and manage money and relationships. This mix of theory and practical advice is the springboard for making sure that money is not a point of conflict in your family and might actually become an area that helps your family connection become even stronger.

2

Discovering Your Money Personalities

When we talk to others about their Money Relationships, we're more interested in the "relationship" part than the "money" part. Money is a tool, a means to an end. And that end is always the relationship.

You spend money on your spouse to demonstrate your love for him or her. You save money for your children's educations to help launch them into adulthood. You set aside money for your retirement because you want to relax and enjoy time with your friends and family. You invest to make sure your future is well funded.

Even when you argue about money, you're really fighting about the relationship. One of you feels disrespected by the other. Or you are afraid that your spouse is going to ignore your financial plans and leave you without a nest egg. You argue because you feel misunderstood or ignored. When you get mad at your partner for buying $100 shoes after agreeing that you could only afford to spend $50, it's not the extra $50 that bugs you. It's that this person you love and trust violated your agreement.

This idea that your relationship matters more than your money is central to what we're talking about in this book. You have a Money Relationship with your partner, but you also have a Money Relationship with each of your children. And we know that you want to make that relationship as strong and healthy as possible, not because you hope your kids will save 30 percent of their allowance or know how to calculate interest, but because you treasure your connection with your kids.

But so often, we meet families who are struggling to keep that connection strong because of money. Mom and Dad disagree about how much allowance little Zack ought to get and what he should do to get it. Now that she has her first job, Candace can't keep a buck in her pocket, and her seeming irresponsibility drives her parents crazy. Ben is a sophomore in college and can't get his credit card debt under control, no matter how much his parents harp on him about it. In all of these cases, the Money Relationships between parents and their kids is starting to crack. And no one is happy about it.

That's why it's essential that parents not only have the practical tools to talk about the nitty-gritty details of money management but also have the kind of relationship tools that help keep them close and connected with their kids.

And the best tool of all is understanding something we call your Money Personalities.

We all know people who have very different ideas about

money than we do. It doesn't take long to rattle off a list—your buddy who can't wait to show you his latest purchase, the friend who clips coupons and outfits her kids with thrift store finds, the coworker who's always playing the stock market and the one who gets nervous every time the market takes a dip. And then there are those people we know who don't seem to care about money at all. Spend it, don't spend it—they don't give it a second thought.

What we've come to see in our years of working as financial advisors is that everyone has his or her own unique way of thinking about and dealing with money. And those particular ideas are what make up a person's two Money Personalities.

We (Scott and Bethany) happen to have lots of similar ideas about money. We both love to spend, spend, spend. Our family vacations are a blast! We don't even care if we spend a lot of money. When we were first married and working hard to get our financial footing as a couple, we would still find ways to scratch that spending itch. It could be a stop for ice cream on the way home from work or a weekend getaway or finding just the right gift for a friend or even donating a good chunk of money to a cause we were passionate about. It has never been about the stuff for us, but about the enjoyment we get from spending.

So when we meet people who love to save money, those people who would rather wear a ten-year-old suit than splurge on something new or who will shop for day-old bread just to save a dollar or two, well, we don't get it. And those people who don't think about money at all? What planet did they fall off of?

You have two Money Personalities, your parenting partner has two Money Personalities, and each of your kids has two Money Personalities. While you might have some shared ideas about money, it's highly likely that you also have many differences in your Money Personalities. It's those differences that create tension in your Money Relationship.

Remember, almost every decision you make has a money component to it, so the way you think about and deal with money has a huge impact on your daily life and your interactions with other people. That's why it's so crucial to know your Money Personalities and to figure out your children's Money Personalities.

So let's get to it!

There are five basic Money Personalities:

Saver

The Saver loves to save money and gets a huge thrill out of getting a good deal. Whether he has loads of money or barely a penny to his name, the Saver is always looking for ways to spend less. Savers love to save money and also get pure enjoyment out of helping others save money too.

Spender

It's no surprise that the Spender is all about the enjoyment that comes from spending money. It doesn't matter if she's spending on herself or giving to others. It doesn't have to be a lot—the thrill of buying a new car isn't all that different from the thrill of buying a pack of gum. Okay, maybe it's a little different, but for a Spender, buying is buying, and it's awesome.

Risk Taker

These are the entrepreneurs, the visionaries, the ones willing to put every dime they have into a high-risk venture. They are as likely to end up billionaires as they are to end up bankrupt. But it's their love of adventure, a new deal, or the unknown—not their bank accounts—that drives them.

Security Seeker

Security Seekers are always looking ahead and thinking about the plan for the future. The strong sense of planning gives them the secure feeling they need.

Flyer

This is the most unusual Money Personality of all. Flyers fly by the seat of their pants when it comes to money, because they always put relationships over their money decisions. Money barely registers as something that needs to be considered. They rarely talk about money, think about money, or care about money.

Of these five Money Personalities, there will be two that fit you—a Primary Money Personality and a Secondary Money

Personality. Think of these two as a team, partners that work together, balance each other out, and even compete with each other. Sometimes one of your Money Personalities drives decisions; sometimes the other takes over. Once you figure out your Primary and Secondary Money Personalities, ask your parenting partner to do the same.

You can look over this list and know fairly quickly your Primary and Secondary Money Personalities. Since this book is focusing on your children, we're going to spend the next chapter talking about Money Personalities as they relate to kids. But all the conversations we're going to cover will go a whole lot better if you and your parenting partner know your own Money Personalities as well.

To confirm your Primary and Secondary Money Personalities, take a few minutes to pop over to our website, TheMoneyCouple.com, and take the Money Personalities Assessment. It's quick, it's easy, and it will be a great help to understanding yourself before working through money issues with your kids.

As the two people who matter most to your children, it's essential that you and your parenting partner approach the conversations that follow as a united team. You might have very different Money Personalities. It's quite possible that you have your own issues when it comes to money. Maybe your marriage ended because of money conflicts. But this is the time to put all of that aside so you can work together to help your kids avoid those same problems and arguments down the road.

In each age and stage section, we'll discuss a few of the "button pushers" that might come up for you as parents when your child's Money Personalities clash with yours. For example, if you're a Spender/Risk Taker and you have a child who's a Saver/Security Seeker, you might be endlessly frustrated by your child's anxiety about saving money and the future. But when you recognize that her anxiety is part of her Money Personality and not some character flaw on her part, you are better equipped to help her deal with those fears objectively and without getting into pointless arguments.

If you and your parenting partner are struggling to get on the same page as a couple or as parents, we highly recommend you check out our book *The 5 Money Personalities: Speaking the Same Love and Money Language* and our website (themoneycouple.com) for some quick resources to help you get past your own issues and start working together. One of the best gifts you can give your children is a great relationship with your parenting partner. It's the best way to give your children a better chance of having great relationships themselves. And because money affects just about every decision you make as a couple, having a strong Money Relationship is a huge part of building a strong partnership. When you model that kind of communication and mutual respect, it will have a lifelong, positive impact on your kids.

Learning how to work through money decisions together is going to go a long way toward reducing tension in your family. It's going to bring you closer together. And it's going to help all of you learn more about yourselves and each other. Plus, it can even be kind of fun.

Kids and Money Personalities

Cassie is fourteen years old and has started a babysitting business in her neighborhood. She has a handful of regular families and has started making some serious cash. That's a good thing, because Cassie loves to shop. However, Cassie's Primary Money Personality is a Saver. So when Cassie shops, she heads straight to the clearance rack or, better yet, her favorite secondhand shop. She hates to pay more than $5 for anything. What she doesn't spend, she keeps in a vintage coffee tin in her room. Once a month she rides her bike (a classic ride she nabbed at a garage sale for $10—a worthwhile splurge) to the bank and deposits her cash in a savings account so when the time is right, she can buy a car. After almost a year of babysitting, she has saved up nearly $2,000.

Even though her Primary Money Personality is a Saver, her Secondary Money Personality as a Spender shows through as well. Her love of shopping reveals her Spender

Money Personality, but the fact that she will hit only the sale racks, loves to shop at thrift stores, and refuses to pay full price reveals her Saver Money Personality.

We've come to believe that your Money Personality is part of your DNA. There's no Money Personality gene, of course, but the way you think about money seems to be something you're just born with. Even family dynamics and history seem to have little to do with our Money Personalities. We've met Spenders who grew up during the Depression and Savers who were raised in very wealthy families.

Our two boys couldn't be more different in their Money Personalities. Our oldest son, Cole, is a Risk Taker/Saver, and our son Cade is a Spender/Security Seeker. If someone gives Cade a few bucks for his birthday, he has figured out before blowing out the candles how he'll spend it. We're both Spenders ourselves, so we totally get it. Cole, on the other hand, will hang on to every cent he has. A few years ago, he told us he wanted to buy an awesome car one day. Scott thought that was a fabulous goal and told Cole that when he was old enough and had a car in mind, we would match any money he saved dollar for dollar. Scott clearly had no idea whom he was dealing with. Today, at age twelve, Cole has more than $2,500 in the bank. If he keeps this up, we'll have to sell our cars and maybe our house to keep our promise.

Both of these boys have grown up with parents who are serious Primary Spenders. But they are wired differently. Our job isn't to mold them into little versions of ourselves. It's to help them make the most out of their unique, God-given Money Personalities.

We've also found that our Money Personalities show

up in other areas of our lives. People with the Risk Taker Money Personality tend to be more adventuresome by nature. Spenders tend to be outgoing and gregarious in their social interactions, not just in their money decisions. How these traits all fit together is part of the mystery of how human beings are put together. But what we know for sure is that our Money Personalities are as unique and innate as the color of our eyes or the shape of our earlobes.

The carryover from Money Personality to general personality is particularly evident in children. They naturally have fewer interactions with money than adults do, so many of the signs of their Money Personalities show up most clearly in behaviors that have almost nothing to do with money. It will take a little extrapolation on your part to figure out your child's Money Personalities. Not every part of the descriptions will match your child, but they should give you a good general understanding of each Money Personality. Good news! We have included in this book a code for kids to take the Money Personalities Assessment.

Please take these descriptions for what they are—an overview of the five ways people think about and deal with money. They aren't the sole defining aspects of your child's personality. And they aren't excuses for disrespect or rebellion. They are meant to be lenses that help you see something new in your children, something that can help you communicate with them about money matters in meaningful ways.

Read these descriptions with your children in mind and figure out each child's Primary and Secondary Money Personality. One will likely be a no-brainer—that's your child's Primary Money Personality. The Secondary Money

Personality will be the one that shows up when your child is anxious about money or excited about it.

We've laid out a few of the strengths and the challenges for each Money Personality. Knowing their Money Personalities is going to help you know your kids in a new way. You might see all of them in your child; you might see only a few. But there's enough here to give you a good sense of how your children think about and deal with money.

Saver

 For the Saver, it is all about the deal.

While Savers don't always save in the same ways, there are some traits that are common to most Savers. Your child is a Saver if she:

- Loves to collect things—rocks, sticks, coins, bottle caps. These collections are a sign that your child likes to keep possessions, a trait that will carry over when she has some money of her own.
- Rarely spends impulsively. Yes, most kids are relatively impulsive—they don't have the long-term sense of cause and effect adults do—but even as children, Savers tend to think through money decisions with more care than their peers.
- Becomes upset when she spends money. She might show signs of anxiety or complain about a headache. You might notice a change in demeanor or a shorter temper. Spending money creates real, physical stress for Savers.

- Hoards her Halloween candy. You can tell a lot about a child by how she treats this influx of sugary goodness. A Saver will do things such as keep her candy in a drawer and eat one piece a day. Or she'll hide it from her siblings and maybe even forget where she put it. She might not eat any of it at all in an effort to avoid running out before next year. The specifics will vary from child to child, but every Saver kid has a big ol' stash of saved candy.

As we said, every Money Personality has its challenges. If your child is a Saver, you need to be aware that she can be:

- Anxious. Savers can be so concerned about losing what they have, they forget to have fun. We know a young Saver who loved to collect rocks at the beach. Once he had a few he liked, he would stop swimming and just sit with his rocks to make sure none of them got lost. His concern for the rocks overtook his love for the water.
- Overly focused on what things cost. When Savers get their hearts set on something—think of Cassie from the earlier example who was saving for a car—they can lose sight of more immediate goals. Cassie often turns down invitations to go to movies or out for pizza with her friends, because she's worried it will cost too much. The girl has a pile of cash in her room, but she's so set on getting that car that she's missing out on the fun that's right in front of her.
- Seen as selfish. Adult Savers often come across as

cheap to their friends. But in children, this need to keep what they have plays out as selfishness. They can be resistant to sharing the things they've bought with their own money or collected themselves. They might get particularly upset when a sibling messes up their room or when you rearrange their stuff. These things push against the Saver's need for control. And that Halloween candy? Good luck getting her to hand over a peanut butter cup.

Savers have a lot going for them. They are great at setting goals—financial and otherwise. They are highly responsible with their money. And they will almost always make smart money decisions. The challenge for Savers is to stay focused on what really matters in childhood—family, friendships, and fun.

Spender

 A Spender's money decisions are all about enjoyment.

Spenders don't care how much they spend or who they spend it on. They don't have to have a lot of money to spend it—we know Spenders who can do some serious shopping at the dollar store. Spenders just like spending. Your child is a Spender if he:

- Craves instant gratification. Spenders have a hard time putting off until tomorrow what can be purchased today.

- Loves to help and share with others. Spenders are typically very generous, not just with their money but with their time and energy. If you have one of those kids who is relatively eager to pitch in or who likes to be part of whatever is going on, he might very well be a Spender.

- Can't get out of a store without asking for something. Most kids have the "gimmes" in the checkout line, but Spenders are relentless. But here's the thing—they don't really care what they get; they just want to get something. It could be a pack of gum, a new toy, a roll of duct tape. It doesn't matter how much it costs or what it is. It's the fun of getting something that compels the Spender.

- Is persistent. A Spender will work on you until he gets a yes out of you. If you say no to the ice cream sandwich, he'll move on to asking for the bag of chips. He'll keep at you until you give in.

- Cleans out his Halloween candy before Thanksgiving. He might not eat it all—he'll happily give some away or even throw it away when he has had his fill. But he won't hang on to it.

If your child is a Spender, you need to be aware that he can be:

- Impulsive. He'll spend his allowance before the day is over. When it comes to spending money, Spender kids have a hard time knowing the difference between wants and needs, so they behave as though everything is equally important.

- Quiet about spending. The Spender's tendency toward impulsiveness means he doesn't think—or talk—through his decisions. This lack of communication can come across as sneaky or secretive to parents, but that's rarely the Spender's intention.

- Prone to shame. Spenders love to spend, but after the rush is over, they can feel a deep sense of loss and regret. A Spender child might blow all of his birthday money on a game only to realize a week later that he really doesn't like it all that much. Or he might give money to a buddy and then feel like he has been taken advantage of. This cycle of spending and remorse can take a toll on a Spender's self-esteem—he'll feel stupid for making a poor choice, or he'll make unrealistic goals for his next windfall. If your child experiences these kinds of ups and downs when it comes to money, he's probably a Spender.

- Broke. We know Spender kids who have great summer jobs and not a dime to show for it come September. We know young Spenders who have spent every cent of their allowances on baseball cards that are now lost in the dark corners of their rooms. If your child has some source of income, such as an allowance or a job, but never seems to have any money of his own, he's probably a Spender.

Spender kids are a lot of fun to have around. They will live life to the fullest and love to give money away. But they need your help developing impulse control and finding the balance between enjoyment and responsibility.

Risk Taker

A Risk Taker's money decisions are all about adventure.

Kids don't have a lot of opportunities to take financial risks—no one's asking a nine-year-old to invest in a start-up company. But it's still pretty easy to spot a young Risk Taker. Your child is a Risk Taker if she:

- Dreams big. Risk Takers tend to be idea people— they are all about having a new and different plan. If your child has all kinds of big ideas for projects and adventures—backyard campouts, epic lemonade stands, trips in her homemade spaceship—she's probably a Risk Taker.
- Is fearless. We all know kids like this. Some of us may have been kids like this. Risk Takers are the ones who build bike ramps off the garage roof and have their first set of stitches before they start elementary school. This lack of fear can really scare parents, but it's a quality that can lead your Risk Taker into incredible opportunities down the road.
- Makes decisions easily. A Risk Taker knows what she wants. She trusts her intuition and doesn't hesitate to act on a hunch. Risk Takers make

friends quickly, because they instinctively zero in on kids they know they'll get along with.

- Loves to wheel and deal. Risk Takers are the kids who get a kick out of trading Hot Wheels or Polly Pockets. They are not attached to their stuff. Instead, they love that feeling of stepping into something different and interesting. That's where the thrill lies.
- Trades her Halloween candy. Every kid does a little of this, but a Risk Taker has the candy shuffle down to an art form. If she plays her cards right, she will end the night with exactly what she wants— nothing more, nothing less. The trade is as much a part of the Halloween experience as the costume and the candy.

If your child is a Risk Taker, you need to be aware that she can be:

- Careless about details. Risk Takers love making plans. Executing those plans? Not so much. So when your child has one of her big ideas, she might get frustrated that it isn't coming together like she thought it would. Or she might expect you to take care of the details even though it wasn't your idea. These are places where conflict can flame up.
- Insensitive. Because Risk Taker kids know what they want and are really excited to get it, they have a tendency to roll right past anyone who isn't on board. That means friends and siblings might get a

little wounded by the Risk Taker's enthusiasm and single-minded search for adventure.

- Prone to real consequences. Risk Takers get hurt—a lot. Adult Risk Takers are often the ones to lose everything they have in one big deal gone wrong. In kids, the Risk Taker Money Personality has more relational fallout than financial risk. They risk losing friends, getting physically hurt, or destroying property, all in their search for that big rush of adrenaline.

Risk Takers have the potential to be world changers. They are often the visionaries who bring about real, lasting progress in business, in relationships, in their finances. But as children, their risky behavior often looks more like insanity and even delinquency. Young Risk Takers need their parents to help them learn to find adventure without leaving a trail of relational wreckage in their wake.

Security Seeker

For Security Seekers, money decisions are all about the future.

We don't see a lot of children who are Security Seekers in a financial sense—kids don't really think about their retirement accounts or long-term investments. But we know lots of kids who are Security Seekers just the same, and they will indeed become adults who think about their retirement accounts—a lot!

Your child is a Security Seeker if he:

- Needs clear expectations. Security Seekers are the kids who like to know what's coming, what you need from them, what the rules are. When they don't have a solid idea of what a situation entails, they get anxious and easily frustrated.
- Craves information. If your child has an encyclopedic knowledge of bearded dragons or volcanoes or the history of the planets, he might be a Security Seeker. These kids like to know stuff. This need to know is their way of coping with the unknown future.
- Understands the power of delayed gratification. Young Security Seekers won't ask for a toy every time you hit the store. At least they won't beg you to get it right that minute. They are perfectly happy to wait until Christmas or their next birthday to get what they want. Security Seekers, like Savers, have no trouble squirreling away their money for a rainy day. The difference is that Security Seekers know exactly which rainy day they are saving for.
- Is always prepared. Boy Scout or not, the Security Seeker is rarely caught without a firm plan for the future. Whether it's knowing just which sweatshirt he's bringing to camp when camp is still two months away or knowing which three colleges he's applying to even though he's only thirteen, this is a kid who thinks ahead.
- Has a trustworthy Halloween route planned

out. These kids leave nothing to chance, so your Security Seeker will likely go to only houses and neighborhoods he knows well. And he will probably be happy to part with candy he has never tried before while hoarding his favorites.

If your child is a Security Seeker, you need to be aware that he can be:

- A worrier. Security Seekers deal with a lot of anxiety, because the future really can't be totally planned out. So you might find that your child hesitates to participate in new activities or gets especially nervous at the start of a school year. These are all signs that he wants more information and your assurance that things will work out.
- Indecisive. Even with all their prep work and planning, Security Seekers can have a hard time actually putting their ideas into action. They worry that the reality might not be what they expected, that they might have forgotten some important detail, that they might be caught unprepared.
- Inflexible. Security Seekers get anxious when plans change, so you might find your child says no to new plans or spontaneous ideas.
- Controlling. In his efforts to keep his anxiety at bay, the Security Seeker can limit the creativity and ideas of other people, especially his friends and siblings. He might take over the fort-building project from his sister because he thinks he has

better ideas for making it work. He might resist the efforts of his more adventuresome friends and try to push them into activities he likes instead.

Security Seekers will always have a plan. And that makes them a great asset to your family. But they can also err on the side of being too cautious and missing out on the crazy adventures that make childhood so much fun.

Flyer

 For the Flyer, money decisions are all about the relationship.

The Flyer is a great Money Personality, because Flyers don't really think about money at all. That's why on the surface, most kids look like Flyers, especially in their elementary years when they don't naturally understand money well. But just like the other Money Personalities, this one shows up in lots of ways that will help you figure out if your child is just being a kid or really is a Flyer. Your child is a Flyer if she:

- Goes with the flow. Flyers are fairly comfortable with change, even sudden change. Planning to go to a movie and decide to stay home for game night instead? No problem for the young Flyer. Flyers are far more concerned with their relationships than their activities.
- Hates feeling controlled. The one area where Flyers will push back is when they feel as though their

relationships are being restricted. So your young Flyer might get upset when a playdate falls through or when you limit the time she can spend texting her friends. You can limit her screen time, limit her iTunes purchases, limit her allowance, and she won't bat an eye. But limit her time with friends, and she'll put up a fight.

- Is all about the here and now. Flyers aren't too concerned about the future. While parents might see this as a problem, it actually serves Flyers very well. They don't get anxious about things they can't control, and they rarely worry about much beyond their friendships and family connections. That makes them wonderful to be with. They are completely focused on the people around them.

- Will do anything for a friend. Flyers might not have a clue about money, but they are relationship pros. They are deeply caring and generous with their time and affection and will happily set aside other commitments if a friend needs help. They are loyal, compassionate, and as good a friend as you're likely to find.

If your child is a Flyer, you need to be aware that she can be:

- Flaky. Because relationships come first for Flyers, they will sometimes forget about other obligations. You can ask your Flyer to fold the laundry or wash the dishes or walk the dog, but if a friend wants to play or a buddy is calling, well, the dog's going to be disappointed.

- Disinterested in money. This is an understatement. You might have all kinds of great systems and charts and ideas for helping your teenager balance her checkbook or your eight-year-old keep track of her birthday money, but they aren't going to stick with a Flyer. They just aren't motivated by money, so they aren't likely to care one way or the other if they have it or manage it well. Instead, they need relational connections to the lessons you're trying to teach them.

- Un-responsible. To those of us who aren't Flyers, they can look completely irresponsible. They forget their chores, they make impulsive decisions, they don't want to work hard. But the reality is that Flyers have their own priority system, and it rarely involves money. They will gladly clean the bathroom if you or one of their siblings hangs out with them while they do it. They will make solid decisions if they can talk those decisions through with a friend or a parent. And they will work as hard as anyone as long as they don't have to work alone.

Flyers are delightful people. They are laid-back and easy to get along with. But parents can get frustrated by what can often seem to be a lack of drive or focus. That's why Flyers need help finding ways to keep their relationships strong even as they learn how to deal with money in responsible ways.

Now that you've read through these descriptions, your kids' two Money Personalities should make sense. In the chapters that follow, we home in on specific ways to help your children make smart money decisions that take advantage of their Money Personality strengths and help them avoid the pitfalls that their Money Personalities can bring.

At the end of each of the next three sections is a chapter that lays out financial goals for that section's age group. While our major focus is on helping you build a strong Money Relationship with your children by understanding their Money Personalities, we also want to offer some suggestions for concrete financial goals that will help your child become more balanced in his approach to money decisions.

We have a saying that we use when we talk to groups about Money Relationships and Money Personalities: Make It Happen. We use it because it's so easy for people to read about or hear about these ideas and nod and agree that it all sounds really great. But we don't want you to just agree with these ideas. We truly want you to take them, make them your own, and use them to change the way you and your kids talk about money decisions. We want you to reframe the way you think about money, to dig into these Money Personalities, and to understand yourself, your parenting partner, and your kids in a deeper way. In short, we want you to Make It Happen!

Congratulations! Now you know the basics of all five Money Personalities. You also understand that your kids have a Primary and a Secondary Money Personality.

Now you're ready to discover your kids' unique Money Personalities. This code gives you access to the scientific assessment, but more importantly it unlocks your child's money perspective and opens your ideas to his or her unique approach to money.

Select the correct assessment based on your child's age (there are three ranges), and jump right in. (It's perfectly fine to assist your younger children.)

Get started:

1. Find your unique scratch-off access code on the nonprinted side of the cover. It will be covered with foil that you will have to scratch off, revealing the code. Please note that the book will not be returnable once the foil has been scratched off.
2. Go to TheMoneyCouple.com and enter your code to take the Kids' Money Personalities Assessment.
3. Complete the registration process. (We treat your information with the utmost care and security. It is never sold or shared.)

4. Once the registration is complete, you will be taken to the assessment. To allow for multiple children in different age groups, five tests are available with each code. If you require more than five, let us know at info@ TheMoneyCouple.com.

5. If you encounter any issues, you can e-mail us at info@TheMoneyCouple.com.

SECTION 2

· · ·

Ages 5–12

4

Inside the Mind of Your Child

Casey is twelve years old and on the brink of ado-lescence. She is moody, stubborn, and completely unpredictable. One day she wakes up her usual happy-go-lucky self and two hours later she's an emotional basket case. Casey has two younger siblings—an eight-year-old brother and a six-year-old sister—both of whom seem to drive her to the end of her patience far more quickly than they used to.

Casey's parents have considered having Casey do some light babysitting for them—a half hour watching her siblings while Mom runs an errand, maybe watching a movie with the younger kids so Mom and Dad can go out for a short dinner date, that kind of thing. They feel as though it would be a good way for Casey to take on some new responsibilities and earn a little spending money in the process.

But with Casey on this prepuberty emotional roller coaster, her parents are starting to reconsider. They aren't sure they can trust her to be kind to her brother and sister, who are sure to test their sister's limits since they see how easy it is to rile her up. They're not sure which Casey will show up at any given moment—the easygoing, fun-loving Casey or the high-strung, irritable Casey.

On top of these mood swings, Casey is also starting to freak out about money. She has been getting an allowance for a few years and has a little money in a savings account. But as she has gotten older, she has started to ask for more spending money—$10 to go see a movie with some friends, a few bucks to download some songs from iTunes, $5 here, $5 there. When her parents try to talk to her about all the money she's spending, she shuts down and storms off to her room, accusing them of treating her like a baby.

Casey's parents are at a loss for how to untangle the various emotional threads that make up their days with a preteen. How much of what they are dealing with is typical prepuberty hormone shifts and how much is just Casey? And as they look at the money decisions that are increasingly part of their daily conversations with their daughter, they wonder how much of the conflict and tension they're experiencing is due to their various Money Personalities.

When we talk about Money Personalities in children, we have to couple that knowledge with some general ideas about the basic developmental issues kids face at each age and stage. This age group in particular covers a huge range of developmental shifts and milestones. As every parent knows, a five-year-old is a very different human being than a twelve-year-old.

But there are some basic developmental principles that do apply to this whole age range. For the most part, kids in this stage are busy shaping their sense of themselves. They are learning what they like, what they're good at, what they think about things. They are practicing a lot of the skills they will hone in their teen and young-adult years—how to manage their emotions, how to navigate relationships, how to express their needs and wants appropriately. They are gaining little bits of freedom and independence and testing their limits.

Unlike the teenagers they will be soon, kids at this stage aren't necessarily pushing back at their parents as they push limits. Instead, they test themselves; they want to know what they are capable of.

All of this translates into how they make money decisions. For kids in this age group, money is like a new toy. It's the ticket to freedom, to stuff, to fun, to growing up. That's why no matter what combination of Money Personalities your child has, you'll find that he has a lot of emotional investment in money decisions at this age. That can make it challenging to have calm, rational conversations about money with your five- to twelve-year-old.

At the same time, because kids at this age have such an emotional connection to money decisions, they are ripe for learning from you. This is the time to build a truly solid foundation for making good financial decisions that make the most of the strengths in your child's Money Personalities and help minimize the potential challenges those Money Personalities present.

Looking back at Casey's family from the beginning of

the chapter, it's clear that part of what's happening with Casey is developmental. She is on the cusp of puberty, a phase that's no picnic for anyone in the family. So her emotions are amplified, and she's easily frustrated.

She's also at an age where she wants her parents to see her as someone who is growing up. She wants to be treated as a mature, smart, responsible young woman, even though she and her parents know she's not quite as responsible and mature as she would like to think. But a lot of her irritation at her parents and siblings is the result of the tension she feels at living with one foot in childhood and one just about ready to jump into the teen years.

Along with these developmental issues, Casey is a burgeoning Spender/Risk Taker. For the first time in her life, she has opportunities to spend money independently, and she's really excited about it. She goes places without her parents and has a little taste of how great it feels to make her own money decisions. The last thing she wants is her parents clamping down on this newfound independence.

What Casey needs most from her parents right now is patience and understanding. If they expect her to make rational decisions about money, they're going to be frustrated. If she expects them to let her do whatever she wants, she's going to be frustrated. But there is plenty of middle ground here for Casey and her parents to work with as they try to find ways for all of them to get what they really need right now.

We'll use the next few chapters to show you specific ideas for talking about challenges like these with your kids. But first, there are a handful of basic developmental themes to keep in mind as you work through the most common money conflicts with your child.

They Want to Be Good at Things

As kids in this age group discover their abilities and interests, they are developing a fundamental set of beliefs about who they are. This is the age when kids love to master new skills. This is why kids in this age range are like mini Cliff Clavins who can spout endless facts about the most mundane topics—dinosaurs and Pokémon characters and baseball stats. They love to know stuff, and they love to tell you about it.

Kids at this age are also surprisingly competitive and hard on themselves. For the first time in their lives, they are kind of coordinated, their bodies finally do pretty much what they want them to do—run without tripping, catch a ball, juggle, dance—and they expect to be good at everything right away. So they can quickly become little perfectionists who beat themselves up when they aren't the best at something or when they discover they don't have the natural abilities they hoped they would have.

This desire to master skills and ideas plays into their sense of self. A child figures out that she's good at sports, or math, or DS games, or tap dancing. She learns that she likes meeting new people or hates to talk in class. She figures out that she's funny or that she can boss her siblings around. These little discoveries weave together into her ideas about who she is and what she's capable of.

All this translates to how kids deal with and think about money at this age. As they do with everything else, five- to twelve-year-olds are trying to figure out if they are good at making money, good at saving money, good at spending money. Remember, money equals growing up, so they want to be seen as people who can make good decisions about this very important new resource in their lives. In other words, they want you to see them as capable and smart about their money.

The tricky part is that their version of "capable and smart" probably doesn't look like yours. But more than anything, your child needs you to see her as someone who is capable of making good money decisions, even if she's not doing things exactly the way you think she should. The worst thing you can do at this stage is to take control of your child's limited financial freedom or belittle his attempts to exercise some independence. When you as the parent take over, you send the message to your kids that they aren't capable, that they don't have the right skills. And for kids at this developmental stage, that's a deeply hurtful message.

Remember, they want to be great at everything, including money decisions. They want to impress you and have you think they are smart and clever and fantastic. So look for ways to praise their effort and help them learn from their mistakes and start over next time. A little patience on your end will go a long way toward building trust between you and your child.

They Are Concrete Thinkers

This is a challenge for a lot of parents. We are great at abstract ideas, at thinking about the future, at imagining all the ramifications of a decision. Kids are not good at any of this. In fact, they really aren't able to do these things until they hit puberty. That's when the brain starts to manage abstract ideas and make sense of cause and effect.

This inability to think abstractly is part of why kids in this age range make what seem to us as parents to be shortsighted decisions—they can't think through the consequences or imagine a future more rewarding than the present. It's not a character flaw; it's how they are wired.

That's why money conversations with kids in this age group need to be as concrete as possible. It's fine to talk about saving money or spending wisely, but you need to give your kids solid reasons for doing so—saving for a rainy day means nothing to a ten-year-old. Saving toward a concrete goal like a new bike, however, means a lot.

They Are Morphing

No matter what challenges you experience as you talk with your elementary-age kids about money, keep in mind that they are not done developing, not by a long shot. You still have plenty of time to identify challenges that might come with their Money Personalities and find ways to help them be more balanced in their money decisions. If your child is careless with her money right now, start working up simple ways to keep track of it. If he's stingy, help him find opportunities to give to others. But be prepared to have the conversations discussed in this section more than once—as your child grows and changes, the challenges he faces when it comes to money will change too.

Your child's developing personality is exactly what makes this such a great time to start building money skills. Your child can practice good habits now, without suffering much from his money mistakes. You'll want to pull your hair out when he trades his new gaming system for a cruddy old set of no-name baseball cards. We get that. But if you can find a way to get over your frustration and dig into the reasons he thought it was a good idea, you can discover more about the way your child thinks. That information can guide you as you help him learn how to make better decisions about money.

Allowance

Tammy and her kids are halfway through their Target run when ten-year-old Alex says, "Mom, can I go *look* at the LEGOs?"

"Sure," says Tammy. "We'll be in the dog food aisle. Come back in five minutes."

"Okay," says Alex as he rounds the corner and heads to the toy section.

Five minutes later, Alex is back—and he has a box in his hands.

"What is that, Alex?" asks Tammy.

"It's that X-Wing Starfighter kit I told you about."

"Alex, that costs almost fifty dollars. We're not buying that."

"But Mom, I brought my allowance money. I can pay for the whole thing!"

"That's not the point, Alex. The point is you're not spending all of your allowance money on that."

"But Mom, it's my money!"

You can see where this conversation is heading, can't you?

If your family uses an allowance system to teach your kids about the connection between work and rewards, you probably have worked really hard to develop a system for helping your kids earn money. Maybe you have a chore chart that has been fine-tuned over the years. Maybe you have stickers and job jars and savings goals and so many great ideas you could fill up a Pinterest board. And then, bam! One trip to the store and the whole thing falls apart with the emotional meltdown of a ten-year-old.

We're big fans of giving kids an allowance. There's no better way to help kids learn a number of valuable financial lessons about responsibility, hard work, and the value of a dollar. Allowances give kids a sense of ownership over their money and let them have some say-so about what they do with it. Allowances are a great tool for helping kids gain invaluable experience with saving and spending and giving.

But allowances can also bring about some serious money conflicts between parents and kids, especially if you have different Money Personalities. Even if your system for distributing allowances is fairly foolproof, it won't help you deal with the emotional side of money decisions. And it's those emotions that can have the biggest impact on your relationship with your kids.

That's really the focus of these conversations. The financial details—how much your child gets, what she has to do to earn her allowance, how often she gets paid—are really a matter of family preference, and you won't hurt your children if your system is different from someone else's. But what *will* hurt your whole family is if allowances become a point of contention between you and your kids.

If you don't have a workable system for allowance and you want to use this method of teaching financial skills to your kids, we encourage you to head to our website for suggestions on creating a plan for giving your kids an allowance. For now, we want to focus on ways to strengthen the Money Relationship you have with your kids.

The money conflicts and challenges that arise around allowances will vary depending on your child's Money Personalities. We've broken down the potential issues by Money Personality. So think about your child's Primary and Secondary Money Personalities. Keep in mind that the Primary and Secondary Money Personalities work as partners—sometimes you'll see more of one than the other. Then read our suggestions for taking those Money Personalities into account as you talk with your child about allowances.

Here's how to talk to your:

Saver

 Remember that kids at this age want to be good at things. They love to show off their mastery of information and new skills. This developmental need shows up in a big way for Savers. They are so proud of their ability to save money, and they want you to be proud of them too. So if you have a Saver, be sure to praise his ability to save his money. It really is a great attribute and will serve him well as he gets older.

But the challenge with Savers is that they tend to hoard their money. They won't spend it, they won't share it, and they won't necessarily have a plan for what they want to do with it. Savers just like having that money and knowing it's not going anywhere.

Your Saver also likes the sense of control that comes with saving money. That's why he's likely to get upset or anxious when you suggest he spend his money on a gift for his sister or tell him he'll have to buy his own baseball cards. He might do those things on his own, but he wants to be the one making those decisions.

Savers also struggle with having a clear picture of their financial reality. They tend to think they have little or no money, that they are about to run out, when in fact they have a healthy stash tucked away somewhere. If your child is a Saver, ask him how much he has. Either he will know exactly—to the penny—how much he has saved up or he'll give you a number that's well below his actual savings. Either way, there's an underlying concern that he has limited resources and he's reluctant to let any of it go.

You can help ease some of your Saver's anxiety about money by giving him a visual way to track his income and outflow. Older kids might do well with a chart or even a journal that can act as a kind of ledger. Have your child make four columns on the page—one for income, one for savings, one for giving, one for spending. He can use this chart to keep track of where his money is going, and you can use it to help him see how much money he really has.

Young children can use an even more visual way of tracking their money. Give your child three small envelopes or buckets or boxes—one for spending money, one for savings, and one for giving. Every time you hand out her allowance, help her decide how much should go in each envelope or bucket, making sure she puts something in each one.

Regardless of your child's age, your young Saver will need constant encouragement to avoid letting money be more important than relationships. If a friend asks her to go to the candy store but she hesitates because she doesn't want to spend money, have her take a look at her actual cash on hand and figure out how much she would feel comfortable spending on candy. Help her see that saving money is a tool—by saving money on things that don't matter to her, she has money to spend on things like a candy run with a friend—but that saving her allowance for the sake of having more money isn't a healthy goal.

Spender

 For young Spenders, there is no time like the present to use that allowance money for some great purchase. Spenders know how to embrace every moment, and money is their ticket for doing just that. Add in the fact that kids at this age aren't ready to think abstractly, and you have a potential spending nightmare on your hands.

You might also find that your Spender runs through his allowance in record time, not because he's buying stuff for himself but because he's bankrolling his whole group of friends. We know Spender kids who think nothing of paying for all of their friends to go out for a milkshake or a movie. Spenders are generous—sometimes to a fault—and will happily be the bankroll for any activity or endeavor their friends come up with.

This is one of those Money Personalities that can lead to all kinds of conflicts between parents and children. If you're not a Spender, your child's habits can seem careless and irresponsible. And if you are a Spender, you might still find yourself frustrated by the lack of balance between your child's spending habits and his ability to save anything. These conflicts make it highly tempting to tell your child he's reckless or immature, to try to take control over his spending, or to cut off his allowance completely.

Keep in mind that your Spender child really likes being a Spender. He likely sees himself as a generous friend, a fun kid, and a person other people like being with. And he's right! He's probably all those things. So if you become critical of his spending, well, he's going to take that personally.

The key for helping a Spender learn good habits is to work with those great qualities—the generosity, the love of a good time, the joy he gets from giving gifts and treating his friends. When your Spender sees his allowance as a means for doing good in the world, he's going to get on board with any money plan you help him create.

We suggest a three-pronged approach. First, the savings plan. Spenders are very "here and now" in their thinking, so they need you to nudge them into some delayed gratification. When talking with Spenders, we prefer to replace the term *savings* with *future spending plans*. For Spenders, this subtle shift in language helps them see the future as an opportunity to do something cool with their money. And that will make them more inclined to set aside a chunk of their allowance every week. So get your child thinking about something he wants—a new bike, a cool LEGO set, an art kit. Figure out how much it costs, and determine how much he'll need to set aside each week or month to get that item. The ability to set a money goal and discipline himself to meet it will be one of the best financial skills he can develop.

Next is the giving plan. The generous nature of Spenders makes this a pretty painless process—they are happy to give their money away. But you can instill a sense of intention and charity in your child by helping him choose a cause that's meaningful to him. When Bethany was diagnosed with breast cancer a few years ago, our Spender son, Cade, started giving a bit of his allowance to a charity that raises money for breast cancer research. That personal connection between his giving and something that was happening in our lives made it easy for him to set aside that money every week. If your child plays soccer, maybe he can contribute to a charity that sends soccer balls to kids in poor countries or that helps fund a sports program for low-income kids in your area.

Finally, your child needs a spending plan. Obviously, this will be pretty easy for the Spender. But instead of just handing over his allowance and telling him he can do whatever he likes with the chunk set aside for spending, ask him to talk through purchases with you. If you know he buys nachos for the whole crew every time they go to the pool, have him take only enough money for himself so he doesn't become the default sugar daddy. But do your best to give him a good bit of freedom with his spending. If he's keeping up with the savings and giving goals you've set together, he needs to have the freedom to do what he wants with his spending money, even if he sometimes makes choices you're not crazy about.

Risk Taker

 A young Risk Taker doesn't have many chances to take actual financial risks, so it's easy to miss some of her more challenging Money Personality traits. At this age, a lot of Risk Takers look like Spenders or Savers. But you might notice that your Risk Taker wants to save her money for something unusual, like a chemistry set, or that she wants to spend her money on a video camera so she can make movies with her friends. She's not interested in having things—she's interested in experiences. That's a Risk Taker, through and through.

When it comes to using his allowance wisely, the biggest hurdle for your young Risk Taker will be that he isn't quite able to think through the consequences of his decisions. This is partly because of his age and developmental stage, but his Risk Taker Money Personality adds another level of impulsiveness to the mix.

You can counter this lack of future thinking by being overt about your expectations for your Risk Taker's spending and savings plans. You can honor your child's love of new and different experiences by helping him set savings goals that give him those experiences he craves. Maybe he wants to ride the biggest roller coaster in the state before he turns ten. Saving up enough for admission to that theme park is a perfect short-term savings goal for a Risk Taker.

As your Risk Taker gets a bit older, help him look further down the road for his savings goals—maybe he can start saving for a cool vintage car. Maybe he can start setting aside money to fund a backpacking trip after his high school graduation. When he knows there's an incredible experience waiting for him, your Risk Taker will be much more inclined toward smart spending and saving.

Security Seeker

 Security Seekers are all about the future, and that makes them great planners, especially when it comes to money decisions. They are willing to forgo fun now if it means less stress in the future. If your Security Seeker sets money aside for something, like vacation souvenirs or a special toy, you can bet she will hang on to that money and spend it exactly the way she planned to.

But even with their great ability to plan and save for the future, young Security Seekers can feel anxious about the future. Your Security Seeker might not think about the future in financial terms just yet, but she might be thinking about where she'll live when she grows up or what kind of job she wants or coming up with a plan to live with her best friend. Every child thinks about the far-off future, but for Security Seekers, these thoughts aren't vague ideas—they are real concerns.

When it comes to her allowance, you might find that your Security Seeker has lots of plans for her money, but that few of those plans involve spending it anytime soon.

Even if you have a solid spending/saving/giving plan set up, she might be resistant to spending her money, because she would rather just save it all toward her goal.

That's why Security Seekers need both short-term and long-term savings goals. And when we say short-term, we mean no more than a few months down the road. Your Security Seeker doesn't need to save huge chunks of money, but help her practice saving up $20 or so for a certain toy or experience. This shows her that it's okay for her to let go of some of her money now and then and that she'll still have enough for her other plans.

The same is true with giving. Your Security Seeker won't be inclined to give money away, so help her get used to the idea with a $5 donation here and a $10 donation there. Even saving up some of her change to drop in the Salvation Army kettle can get her in the habit of sharing what she has while knowing she's not going to ruin her plans for the future. And when she knows that's the plan, she'll do a great job of making sure it's exactly what happens.

Flyer

 The fact is that most kids act like Flyers on occasion. They don't have the skills to save well or spend responsibly, so they often look like they just don't care about or think about money. But a true Flyer child won't care if he gets an allowance at all. He won't remind you that it's payday. He won't ask for extra chores so he can earn money for a cool toy. He simply won't think about it at all.

If your Flyer child does get an allowance, the challenge is to help him be thoughtful about what he does with that money. Unlike the other Money Personalities, the Flyer doesn't have a need to control his spending or his savings. He will be perfectly happy for you to take over and just tell him what to do. As tempting as that might be, these years are the perfect time to help your Flyer develop a few money-management skills.

Those lessons will only stick if you keep in mind that the key to your Flyer's attention is relationships. The more you can tie money goals and decisions to relationships, the deeper those messages will sink into your Flyer. So ask your child an open-ended question like, "What would you do if you had a hundred dollars?" Then listen carefully. Your child might tell you about a fun experience he would like to share with his friends or about someone he would like to help out. At the core of his thoughts will be a relational goal.

As you work with your child over the coming weeks and months, remind him of those dreams he talked about. He doesn't have to save $100 or do exactly what he said he would do with this imaginary money, but he should think of some manageable goals for his saving and giving. Keep connecting his efforts to the relational side of those goals—say something like, "Won't it be fun when we take your friends to the amusement park next month?" or "I just know those kids at the children's hospital are going to have a great time with the toys you're going to donate."

And pay attention to your Flyer's spending. Until he gets a little older and has a few more money skills, you might need to hold the purse strings for this child. Even adult

Flyers have a hard time keeping track of their money, so a young Flyer will need a little more adult supervision on his spending than a young Saver. If your Flyer is going somewhere with friends, give him only enough money to pay for the movie or the candy or the pool fee and no more. If you hand him a $20 bill, you're never going to see the change.

Button Pushers for Parents

In all of these conversations, you are likely to experience some tension, especially when your Money Personalities differ from those of your children. We've put together a few tips for each Money Personality to make sure your money conversations with your kids don't get derailed when they start to push your buttons.

Saver

 If you're a Saver, your kids' allowance can be a bumpy road. You will automatically want to crack down on the savings part of your child's allowance, because that's where you are comfortable. That will work out great if your child is also a Saver, but if she has any of the other Money Personalities, her plans—or lack of them—will drive you nuts. So keep in mind that control and mastery are a big deal to your child at this age. You want to make the most of that by being a great teacher who can pass on your saving skills and help your child build those good habits. At the same time, check yourself when you feel your anxiety rising. Do you really need to crack down on your child's spending or risk-taking, or is it just your Money

Personality talking? Try to let your child have the freedom to make her own decisions, even if they aren't the ones you would make. If you hold on too tightly or insist your child do things your way, she is likely to rebel or start keeping secrets from you. And that will be the end of what could be a strong Money Relationship.

Spender

We're both Spenders and our older son is a Saver. So we know firsthand that when your child has a Money Personality that's the opposite of yours, there is bound to be tension. Getting our son to part with his allowance is like trying to get a pit bull to give up a hunk of steak. But remember that our kids want us to see the good in their goals, in their ways of doing things. So even when your child seems like a miser to you, look for ways to acknowledge the smart decisions he's making with his money. At the same time, when you make a purchase you feel good about or when you give money to a great cause, tell your child about it and help him see the joy you experience and share with others when you are generous with your resources.

Risk Taker

If you're a Risk Taker, you'll likely struggle with the Saver, Security Seeker, and Flyer Money Personalities. You'll want them to do something that will make their allowance money grow—a lemonade stand or some other moneymaker. But they will push back and resist, so choose your battles wisely.

If you want your child to practice investing his money in, let's say, a lawn-mowing business, then walk him through the process and talk openly about when to take a risk and when to be a little more careful. Your Risk Taker Money Personality is an awesome asset in teaching your kids how to earn some extra money, but be careful about pushing them when there's a chance they could lose money. While your Money Personality can roll with those losses, other Money Personalities can't.

Security Seeker

 As a Security Seeker, you're always thinking about the big picture—saving for college, building your retirement fund, buying a car for your child one day. But kids, especially at this stage, live completely in the present. So avoid passing on your anxiety about the future to your children. They won't see it as care and concern for them but, rather, as you getting worked up about nothing. And that can be a huge source of conflict for parents and kids. Instead of acting out of anxiety, use your planning skills to help your children set up modest savings goals with their allowances. As they get the hang of it, invite them to pool some of their savings with the money you've already set aside for college or that first car.

Flyer

 If you're a Flyer, you likely don't have an allowance plan set up for your kids in the first place. But if your kids have any of the other Money Personalities, you might find that they have concerns about money that have never occurred to you. It will take some real effort on your part, but it's important that you find ways to nurture your kids' Money Personalities even when they are very different from yours. The good thing is that you don't have to be good at saving money to praise your Saver's or Security Seeker's careful plans. You don't have to love shopping to head to the mall with your Spender for a fun afternoon. Use your love of relationships to find ways to connect with your children and discover more about what makes their Money Personalities tick.

6

The Gimmes

Ed and his daughter, Lizzy, are in the checkout line at the grocery store when Lizzy starts up again.

"Dad, look at this Polly Pocket. I don't have this one."

"I see it, Lizzy. She's very pink."

"Can I get her? Please? She only costs four dollars."

"She costs $4.99, and the answer is no."

"Can I get this sticker book?"

"No, Lizzy. Now stop asking me for stuff."

"Why can't I get something?"

"Because you can't. We need to go."

As they walk out of the store, Lizzy spies the gumball machines in the corner.

"Daddy, can I get some gum?"

Lizzy's got a case of the gimmes.

Those smart folks in retail are the bane of parents everywhere. They put all that stuff at kid height, just begging us to spend another couple of bucks on a little toy or a candy bar or lip gloss or some other trinket that no one needs and only the very strong can resist. Until that glorious day when retailers no longer want us to buy stuff, we parents have no choice but to figure out how to quell the nonstop requests for toys and food and junk that are the by-product of every excursion out of the house.

Then again, you don't have to leave your house for the kids to get a case of the gimmes. Ten minutes of TV will throw at least five must-have products into your child's brain—shoes that light up, dolls that sing along to the iPod, cereal made of candy bars, and who knows what else. On any given morning you'll have three requests for new stuff before you've had your first cup of coffee.

Of all the challenges parents face when it comes to kids and money decisions, the gimmes is probably the hardest, primarily because kids can be relentless in their demands for more stuff. It's the rare parent who can get from the front door of a store to the checkout line without caving in to at least one request for a toy or a new shirt or a bag of chips or a pack of gum. Even the most stalwart Saver can get worn down by the constant nagging from her kids.

Dealing with the gimmes calls for a ton of consistency and discipline on the part of a parent. But it also helps to understand your child's Money Personalities. As with all money decisions and conversations, the more you know about how your child thinks about money, the easier it will be to work through money conflicts and build strong money skills in your child.

Here's how to talk about the gimmes if your child is a:

Saver

If you have a Saver child, throw your hands in the air and shout, "Hallelujah!" The gimmes are a nonissue for this kid. A Saver child doesn't like spending money, even if it's your money. They just aren't tuned in to shopping and getting new stuff. So say thank you to your Saver child. Be intentional about noticing when he doesn't beg you for a toy, when he doesn't ask for one more piece of candy. Tell him you notice and that you appreciate the way he lets you run errands without asking for things. Savers take a lot of pride in their ability to save money, and it means the world to your child when you notice.

If you have other kids who aren't Savers and are able to talk you into the occasional random purchase, you'll also need to make sure you're not unintentionally "punishing" your Saver for never asking for anything. Savers like to save money, but they are also kids who like toys and games and experiences. So give your Saver permission to ask for something now and then, to let you know when she has her eye on something. Help her hunt down good deals on the things she wants or needs. Take her thrift shopping and watch her eyes light up when she gets a deal on a pair of jeans or cute top. Let her know it's okay to spend, not just save, money now and then.

Spender

If your child is a Spender, watch out—these kids just like to get stuff. It doesn't have to be expensive or cool; it just has to be something. Our son

Cade's Primary Money Personality is a Spender, and he will work us until he gets a yes, even on something small at home. He might ask for a cookie. If we say no, he'll ask for a Popsicle. If we say no to that, he'll ask for an apple. And when we say yes, it's like he has won a football game. There's a look of pure victory in his eyes. He doesn't even like apples all that much, but that's not the point. He got something, and that feels great to a Spender. Spenders love the word *yes*!

Your Spender will try his hardest to wear you down. He will ask and ask and ask until you relent. Like Lizzy in the story at the beginning of this chapter, Spender kids will keep at it, knowing that sooner or later you will cave. The only cure for this is for you to stick to your guns and mean it when you say no. Every time you give in, even to a minor purchase like a gumball, you are telling your Spender that you can't resist forever.

So prepare yourself and your child before you head to a store. Remind yourself that you're going to hear lots of requests and decide ahead of time that you're not giving in. Then tell your child something like, "We are getting some groceries, and I am not going to buy anything for you today. Please don't ask me for anything." If your child starts in with the gimmes, remind her that you've already made your decision. Then stick with it. If you can hold to your commitment a few times in a row, you will see a reduction in the requests from your child. They'll know your no means no, and they will eventually stop asking. As you notice fewer requests, be sure to praise your child and let her know that you appreciate the change in behavior. This kind of positive reinforcement goes a long way with a child.

Risk Taker

 Risk Takers have a lot of similarities to Spenders—they're not about to let money get in the way of their awesome ideas. Our son Cole is a Risk Taker/Saver. Not long ago he told us he was saving up to buy an inflatable kayak, and he wondered if we could help him start looking into buying one. We just stared at him, then said, "Buddy, we live in Colorado. The closest lake is two hundred miles away. Where do you think you're going to use this kayak?" He said, "Well, you never know when you'll need one."

For Risk Takers, the gimmes might not be constant, but their requests will often seem unusual, especially if you're not a Risk Taker yourself. You can deal with this by asking your child how she plans to pay for whatever it is she wants. You might be surprised to find that she has a plan that may not even involve your money. (For instance, because he's also a Saver, Cole had his kayak financing already figured out.) But regardless of whose money your Risk Taker wants to spend, she needs your guidance to make sure she's not asking for stuff just to stave off boredom.

Risk Takers have short attention spans when it comes to cool ideas and cool stuff; so if you're not careful, your Risk Taker will end up with a garage full of go-carts and unicycles and build-your-own skateboard ramp projects that get forgotten as soon as the next great idea comes along. If your child seems to jump from must-have to must-have, help focus her need for adventure on experiences instead of material goods. Not only will that keep her from breaking the bank with her latest and greatest purchase but she'll be building relationships and making great memories.

Help your Risk Taker set up a simple savings plan for the stuff she does want to buy. If she's serious about saving up for new Rollerblades or a new game and you want to match her savings, that's fine. But by putting some of the responsibility for getting her hands on cool stuff on her, you'll be helping her avoid the impulse buys and forgotten purchases that can plague a Risk Taker.

Security Seeker

Like Savers, Security Seekers are not really inclined toward the gimmes. They are quick to understand that you can't or won't spend money impulsively. And they have an instinctive understanding of delayed gratification—this is the kind of kid who will start making a Christmas list in May. On those rare occasions when your Security Seeker gets a case of the gimmes, encourage him to add whatever it is he wants to his birthday list or Christmas list. Since Security Seekers are all about planning for the future, this approach will be right in his wheelhouse. Then honor his patience by considering that item as a gift when the time comes. Be vocal about telling him how much you appreciate his contentment with what he has and his ability to wait for something he wants.

Flyer

 The great thing about Flyers is that they aren't hung up on material things. If your Flyer child is begging for a new toy or a new doll, ask her why she wants it. Most of the time, her answer will be based in her relationships—she wants an American Girl doll because her best friend has one and they want to play with them together. She wants that new game because she loves the idea of game nights with the family.

Flyers are all about relationships, so their money decisions are almost always about connecting with the people they love. So when your Flyer has the gimmes, get her talking about the relationship behind her request and help her think about other ways she can make the connections she craves. It won't take her long to move off of the stuff and get back to the relationship.

Dealing with the gimmes is never easy. And we don't mean to suggest that you have to say no to your kids every time they ask for something. If your child wants a gumball and you have no problem buying him a gumball, then knock yourself out. But if you find that you dread taking the kids to the store with you, or if the constant little purchases are creating tension between you and your parenting partner, then use what you know about your child's Money Personalities to make real changes to the way you handle the gimmes. If you stick to your plans, you'll see a difference quickly.

Button Pushers for Parents

Kids are wired to want stuff, so these conversations won't always go smoothly. There might be push back, there might be anger, there might be tantrums—and not always from the kids. If you have different Money Personalities than your kids do, they will find ways to push your buttons. Here's how to avoid your own checkout aisle meltdown.

Saver

 Savers have a major issue with the gimmes. These little requests can add up to big budget breakers, and that makes Savers crazy. For a Saver, a gumball isn't just a gumball—it's the start of the freefall into debt and bankruptcy. Savers also worry that by giving in to the gimmes, they are developing a sense of entitlement in their kids, something every parent tries to avoid. If you're a Saver, acknowledge the fears and anxiety your child's gimmes bring up in you. Then remind yourself about the reality—the occasional impulse buy probably won't break the family budget, and giving good things to your kids just for the heck of it isn't going to turn them into little brats. Say no when you need to, but if you know that you could say yes, then do it once in a while and watch the joy explode on your child's face.

Spender

 If you're a Spender, you probably buy stuff for your kids even when they don't ask for it. But not all Spenders are alike. Some Spenders get irked when it feels like all their kids do is ask for stuff. These Spenders have their own established patterns for buying and often have an internal sense of how much is too much. When you find yourself getting irritated at your kids about the gimmes, take a minute to figure out what's going on. Is it that you feel like a slot machine? Is it that they seem to be asking out of habit and not out of real interest or need? Pay attention to your own frustration, because when a Spender is bothered by the gimmes, it's usually because there's something else going on. When you know what that is, you can better deal with the real issue instead of making it about the spending.

Risk Taker

 When it comes to the gimmes, Risk Taker parents will find themselves frustrated not by the request but by what is being requested. If your child asks for something you deem as boring or a waste, you'll probably say no right away. If she asks for something you think is supercool or interesting, you're more likely to give in. That might not seem like a problem, but if your kids aren't Risk Takers, your reactions can seem random and even hurtful. And that's when the problems start. Keep saying yes to your kids and they will indeed get that sense of entitlement that can make parents crazy. Say no to everything they like and they'll start to take it personally. When your child asks for something, think before you respond and consider why you're about to say yes or no. Make sure you respond based on what's best for your child, not what's most interesting to you. And keep your inner Risk

Taker satisfied by finding ways to create fun and adventure that have nothing to do with purchases or spending a bunch of money. Channel your love of the unknown into spontaneous outings with your kids—a drive to a new playground, a hike in the woods—to show them that adventure doesn't have to cost a thing.

Security Seeker

Security Seekers aren't necessarily tight with their money, but they like to have a plan for their spending. So it's those little purchases, the impulse buys, that get on their nerves rather than planned purchases. This can be confusing for kids—when you take them school shopping, they can buy whatever they need, but when you go to the mall on a whim, they can't. To help your kids understand the difference and avoid the conflicts that come with the gimmes, set clear spending expectations even before you leave the house. If you're planning to spend money, let them know how much. If you're not open to impulse buys, tell them there won't be any requests on this trip. Then stick to the plan once you're out and about.

Flyer

Because they put relationships ahead of money, Flyers have to make sure they aren't being taken advantage of. Even young kids will figure out that Mom or Dad can be talked into anything if they push long enough. If you're a Flyer, you need to be aware of your vulnerability and plan ahead when you take your kids to places where the gimmes are likely to hit. Again, this doesn't mean you have to say no to every request—you're probably happy to buy ice cream cones at the end of your errands, because it means you're making memories with your kids. Just make sure you're agreeing to their requests because you want to, not because you feel pressured.

7

Sports and Extracurricular Activities

Andrew is a great little soccer player. So great, in fact, that at the tender age of eleven he is already being recruited by a club soccer program. After another parks and rec game where he scored five goals, a dad from the other team approached Andrew and his parents. He told them that he coached one of the club teams and that if they wanted Andrew to have a future in high school and college soccer, they needed to get him in the club program as soon as possible. He said, "You know, these high school teams have gotten so competitive that the varsity coaches won't even let kids practice with the team unless they've had at least four years of club time."

Now Andrew is convinced he's the next David Beckham and that his future depends on being part of the traveling team that plays all year and costs, well, a lot more than the parks and rec fall league.

After a little investigating, Andrew's parents learn that being on the traveling club team will cost about $250 for uniforms and fees, and it involves traveling overnight once or twice a month, practicing four times a week, and even making a yearly trip to Texas for a big national tournament.

The whole thing is overwhelming for Andrew's parents. Even if he wasn't already involved in Scouts and karate lessons and volunteering at church on Sunday mornings, the time commitment of traveling to games and practices feels like way too much. And that's not even considering the money. They know the uniform is the tip of the iceberg. There's the gas involved in hauling the family around the state every weekend, the food and hotel costs of those away games, and the big-ticket flight to Texas. One season might very well set them back thousands of dollars.

When Andrew's parents told him they couldn't make it work, he was devastated. They tried to explain that it was too big of a time commitment for them to make and more money than they could afford. But Andrew only heard this: *You're not worth all that money.*

Like so many parents, Andrew's mom and dad are caught between being supportive of their child's interests and talents and letting their time and money get sucked into the great activity vortex. Whether it's sports, dance lessons, Scouts, theater, art classes, band, or youth group, it seems as if activities today take up far more time and money than they did when we were kids. It's a real challenge to find the sweet spot between too much of a good thing and holing up in the house.

This is a tough conversation to have with your child. Here's how to talk through the issues around sports and other activities if your child is a:

Saver

 Even young Savers are very aware that activities cost money. If you are also a Saver, your child has likely picked up on your tendency to look at the cost of an activity before signing on. But even if you don't pay attention to the expense, your Saver child will. It won't always be her primary concern, but you might find that she balks at pursuing her interests because she assumes it will cost too much or it doesn't seem worth the money to her. She will deny herself the joy and fun of doing something she likes for the sake of saving money.

That means you need to give her permission to take a class or join a club. Let her know that you have the money to pay for the activity, you can afford it, you've planned for this expense, and the family will still be able to afford food if she learns how to play tennis. This might sound silly to you if you're not a Saver, but remember that Savers have a good deal of anxiety when it comes to money, and they really do worry about the worst-case scenario.

Now if you honestly can't afford the class or the lessons, let her know and then talk about how she might pursue her interests in other ways. If she wants to learn to paint but art lessons aren't in the picture, talk to the art teacher at school or an artist you might know and get their input. They might have ideas about mentoring relationships or free after-school options you haven't thought of.

Your Saver child will love this process of getting something great for less money, so have her help you do some research and see what options you can come up with. Do your best not to abandon her ideas because of money. Show her that her interests are important to you and worth pursuing, even though money adds a little hurdle.

Spender

 Spender kids won't think twice about the money involved in activities. They might not be aware that their activities cost money in the first place. Not only that, but Spenders love a good time, so they're likely to say yes to all kinds of stuff without really thinking through how it will all fit into their lives. You'll need to pay close attention to your Spender's tendency to sign up and join in. If he comes home and tells you he and his buddies have decided they all want to play baseball, let him know that you need to look into the details. As you do, bring your child into the decision-making process. Help him figure out how he'll make time for all of his commitments. Show him the financial details and, if he's old enough, have him do the math with you to figure out how much all of his activities will cost and whether you can afford them.

These small efforts to help your Spender pay attention to the details of his decisions aren't meant to dampen his enthusiasm. Instead, they will help him develop some discretion and discernment skills he'll need as he gets older. Putting some of the hard work of decision making in his hands gives him that sense of responsibility kids crave, but it also helps him see that when you say no to something, you have good reasons.

Risk Taker

These are the kids who try eighteen activities and stick with none of them. Life for a Risk Taker is all about the unknown—the adventure—and they get bored quickly! They won't think about the money involved. The great side of this Money Personality is that your Risk Taker will have all kinds of interesting, fun experiences. The challenge is to get him to commit to something. Our Risk Taker son, Cole, started karate with all the excitement in the world. But within a few weeks he was over it and ready to move on. We convinced him to stick with it—basically we wouldn't let him quit—and now he has a black belt. That experience has helped him see that there are rewards to committing to something, even when his impulse is to move on.

When your Risk Taker signs up for something or shows an interest in an activity, have an honest talk about whether quitting is an option, and make sure to include the financial facts in this conversation. There will always be activities that aren't the right fit for your child, and there might be times when getting out while you can is the best plan. But for the most part, you need to let your Risk Taker know that if she starts something, she needs to finish it, even if that means she is bored sometimes or doesn't always like it.

And help her understand that the financial aspect of her

decisions is important. Risk Takers don't worry too much about losing money or paying for something they end up not doing. If you're a Risk Taker, too, you might not think much of this either. But if you're not a Risk Taker, it's okay to explain that there are financial ramifications to her decisions. She might not get it, but in time, she'll start to understand that her whims have an impact on the family and that she needs to think a little longer before jumping into her next big adventure.

Security Seeker

 Security Seeker kids are happy to sign up for stuff. They like fun as much as anyone. But they will tend to shy away from new experiences. If she has played soccer for four years, good luck getting her to think about volleyball. If she is a singer, she might be resistant to picking up a dance class. Worries about the unknown can be enough to get your Security Seeker stuck in a rut, taking part in activities even if she doesn't really enjoy them anymore.

The nice thing is that you will almost always be able to plan the financial aspects of your Security Seeker's activities. Since she's not likely to add three new activities to her docket every fall, you'll have a pretty good sense of what her plans will cost you. But even if you like having a fairly stable budget and a good idea of what the year holds in terms of activities, it's important that parents encourage their Security Seeker kids to branch out a bit. If she's not ready to give up soccer, have her at least try playing in a new position or with a few different friends. Do what you can to get her to expand her comfort zone a bit. If she resists, don't push too hard. What matters most is that she's enjoying herself and having good experiences. If she's happy, then let it ride.

Flyer

 Your Flyer child could go lots of directions on the activity issue—if his friends are signing up for something, he will too. If they aren't? Then he'll hang back. Because he is all about relationships, your Flyer might miss out on opportunities to explore his own interests. So make sure your budget includes plans for a handful of classes or lessons or experiences that your child would enjoy; then have him invite a friend to join in. Encourage your child to be the decider at times, instead of just following the whims of his friends.

Because Flyers want to be where their friends are, they can feel awful when they aren't involved in something "everyone else" is doing. So it's important that you not let finances be your primary concern when helping your Flyer choose activities. Of course you need to stick with what you can afford, but make sure your decisions take into account your child's need for connection and relationships. If you can't afford to join the baseball team this year, make plans to go to the game and cheer on the other kids, and find times when your child can hang out with his buddies on non-game days. Make an effort to keep those relationships strong so your Flyer doesn't get left out.

Button Pushers for Parents

The activities question can be tough for parents, because it comes up over and over and over. Holiday money decisions are stressful, but at least they only come around once a year. But sports and activities are year-round. So parents need to be extra in-tune with their own Money Personalities as they navigate these extracurricular decisions.

Saver

 For Savers, "extracurriculars" are just that—*extra*. That means these activities seem like a luxury, and Savers have a hard time making room for luxuries. Plus, the cost of activities and classes is usually set, which means the Saver can't negotiate a discount or a good deal, which is one of the main tools Savers have for making peace with spending money. While it's fine for you to say no to activities that don't fit your budget, make sure you're not saying no just because you hate to spend money. If you can afford to say yes, do it.

If you do need to say no, keep your thoughts about the money side to yourself or at least between you and your parenting partner. Savers can sometimes send the unintentional message to others that money is the most important consideration in any decision. For kids, that message can be very hurtful—especially if your child is a Spender, Risk Taker, or Flyer. It can sound like money is more important than what they want. If you can't afford an activity or feel as though you need to say no, give your child a clear explanation of your reasons. If finances are part of that decision, work with your child to figure out how you can afford it the next time around or come up with other ways to pursue his interest that cost less money. Do what you can to make it clear that you support your child's interests even when you can't afford to put your money where your heart is.

Spender

 The hot button for Spenders is that we say yes to everything! And while that feels great at first, we Spenders know that after a spending fest comes the remorse. We will write a bunch of checks and then, when it's too late to do anything about it, we'll realize we showed no restraint and that we've spent too much or overcommitted our kids. Before long, everyone is tired and starting to resent the activity and each other. Even when money is a nonissue, be careful about saying yes to everything your child wants to do. Sit down together and take a realistic look at the months ahead. What can your family reasonably do? What's going to be too much? What's going to give you the most joy? Seeking a bit of balance will keep activities from becoming a point of contention in the family.

Risk Taker

 For Risk Taker parents, life is an adventure. So you might find yourself frustrated when your child doesn't feel the same way. It might bug you when your child wants to take the same gymnastics class she took last year, or when she has no interest in learning to wake surf over the summer. But Risk

Taker parents need to resist the urge to push their kids into activities they aren't interested in or ready for or that the family can't afford. If you want to wake surf, go for it, but if your child's not into it, let her be.

Risk Taker parents also need to make sure they are encouraging their kids to follow through on commitments. The Risk Taker has no problem moving on from something once it becomes boring, but kids need to learn that when they sign up for something, they have to stick with it. This is important from both a developmental standpoint and a financial one. If your child jumps from activity to activity with your blessing, she learns that the investments of time and money the family is making on her behalf aren't important. And that's when that sense of entitlement can start to grow.

Security Seeker

 Security Seekers have a funny relationship with extracurriculars. For Security Seekers, who are so focused on the future, these kinds of activities are great and totally worth spending money on as long as there is a long-term payoff. So if your child wants to play park league basketball, you might be fine with that until you realize she's not very good and probably won't be getting a Division I scholarship. If there's no future in an activity, it gets harder for a Security Seeker to keep rationalizing spending the money on lessons or teams.

This is why activities can be a surprising hot button for Security Seekers, especially when the kids are young and still exploring their options. If you're a Security Seeker, you need to get comfortable with the idea that your child will be experimenting for a few more years before he finds that handful of activities he really likes. So start making room in the budget now for a class here and a lesson there.

And reframe your focus. The future investment is there, even if your child has no game. The investment in rec basketball might not pay off in college scholarships. All those voice lessons might not lead to a record deal. But the payoff will come in seeing your child find something she loves to do. It will come in the look your child gives you when she looks up in the bleachers and sees you cheering her on. Those are deposits that will pay off forever.

Flyer

 Flyer parents can get their buttons pushed when their children's desires do not provide a connection for the parents. Maybe all your friends are carpooling together as they send their kids to the same camp. But your child wants to go to a different camp, and you'll have to make the drive alone. These concerns can sound strange to a non-Flyer, but if you're a Flyer, you know just what we mean. You tend to check in to see what your friends' kids are doing or what your child's friends are doing before you talk to your child about what he would like to do. As your child gets older and wants more say-so in these decisions, you might find yourself having to let go of your need for connection in order to let your child pursue his interests.

On the money side of these decisions, Flyer parents need to be careful about overcommitting. Like Spenders and Risk Takers, Flyer parents get excited about the potential for newness. In the Flyer's case, it's new relationships and experiences. And that excitement can lead Flyer parents to say yes to more activities than they can afford.

So know exactly what you're willing to spend. And look at the time commitments as well. An overextended family is never a happy family. Make sure you're honoring your family relationships as well as the friendships that come along with activities.

Holidays and Birthdays

Jed's eleventh birthday is a little over a month away, and he knows exactly what he wants to do for his party. Party Zone is the coolest place in town. One of his friends had his party there, and it was awesome! Race cars, laser tag, a batting cage, a huge arcade, miniature golf, pizza, ice cream—everything he loves in one place.

Jed was at that party three months ago, and he hasn't stopped talking about how great his birthday will be when he has all his friends together at Party Zone. He has already told the guys to count on it, that the invitations are coming, and that they are going to have a blast. There's only one problem: Jed's not having a party at Party Zone. It's simply too expensive, and his parents can't afford to spend that kind of money on a birthday party when there are other options available.

Jed is the second oldest in a family of five kids. While his parents make a decent living, they have to watch the budget carefully. Birthday parties are one of the places where they know they need to keep an eye on the expenses. If they have a big Party Zone event for Jed, they will have a harder time convincing his younger brothers and sisters that they need to stick with a party at the house. They have decided they will do one big event party for each child when he or she turns thirteen, but that's it.

They have heard Jed talk about Party Zone, but they hoped he would change his mind after the buzz of his friend's party wore off. It hasn't, and now they need to have a little planning session to reset Jed's expectations and figure out a less expensive plan.

As Jed and his parents talk, it's clear that Jed isn't just upset that he isn't going to have the party he planned on. He is feeling the weight of being a kid in a big family. He has felt it before—only a few Christmas gifts per kid, no spendy school clothes or shoes, not many pizza nights or movies at the theater with the family. Jed knows his parents do their best, but he sees how his friends spend money without thinking twice, how they get to go to the mall or to the amusement park or on big family vacations. And he gets a little jealous.

So when Jed's parents tell him Party Zone is out, all that jealousy comes rushing out. He doesn't ask for much—why can't they do this one thing for him? None of his friends had their parties at home—he will be the lamest kid at school. He hates having a big family and no money. Why do his parents have to be so cheap all the time?

You've probably had more than one experience where

you've dropped your child off at some over-the-top birthday party with jumpy houses or pony rides or make-your-own-stuffed-animal machines. It's like the gauntlet has been thrown and now every parent has been put on notice: if you really love your kid, you had better top this.

The pressure to host a great party is just one of the big money decisions that come along with birthdays and holidays. Parents must also deal with all the birthday parties that their kids are invited to themselves. If your kids have as many friends as ours do, some months seem to have a birthday party every week. All those gifts—even if you have a ten-dollar limit—can add up quickly! And we could write a whole book on dealing with the push to overspend on your kids during the holiday season.

Birthdays and holidays often cause more money conflict for families than all the other money conversations combined, especially when your kids are still in these prime gift-giving years. Birthdays really matter to an eleven-year-old. Christmas gifts really matter to a six-year-old. As kids get older, they are less concerned with having big parties and piles of presents. But at this age, those parties and gifts are a big deal.

That's where the conflict comes in. How can you convince your child that the size of his birthday party has no relation to how much you love him, or that it's okay to get his friends a small gift for their birthdays, or that he really will be as happy with three or four nice presents instead of ten cheap gifts? Understanding your child's Money Personalities can go a long way toward helping you have productive conversations about birthdays and holidays with your child. We suggest having these conversations well ahead of the actual events to help your child adjust his expectations.

Here's how to talk about holidays and birthdays if your child is a:

Saver

 Birthdays and holidays are awesome times to involve your Saver in money decisions. Since Savers aren't inclined to spend a lot of money, they will likely have some great ideas about fun, simple, and low-cost ways to celebrate. This gives them some real ownership of the plans and might even save you some money.

But make sure your Saver isn't denying herself something that's important to her. Some Savers, especially as they get a bit older and start to understand how much things like parties can cost, will say they don't need parties or gifts. As tempting as that might sound, especially if money is tight, don't let your child fall into the habit of sacrificing her own wants and needs for the sake of saving a few dollars. It's okay for her to learn that making memories and having fun with her friends are worth spending money on.

When it comes time for your Saver to buy gifts for others, encourage her to have fun shopping (really, she won't think "fun" and "shopping" go together) for the perfect gift at the dollar store, a thrift store, or garage sales. Help her practice being generous without feeling like she has to spend a ton of money.

Spender

Holidays and birthdays are Spenders' favorite days of the year. It's not only because they will get gifts, although that's always a plus, but also because they get to shop and spend and think about shopping and spending for weeks at a time. Best of all, they have an excuse for shopping! You might find that your Spender is eager to join you in your shopping for everything from birthday decorations to the holiday meal. The rush of finding what you need and bringing it home is always fun for a Spender.

The holidays are a great time to start teaching your Spender how to work with a budget. Show him how you figure out what you can spend on gifts or entertaining; then have him help you comparison shop and find good deals on the things you need. This simple lesson can set the stage for good habits down the line. Adult Spenders often go overboard during the holidays. You can prevent your child from turning into a Spender gone wild with some basic lessons about budgeting now.

When it comes to birthdays your Spender is going to need even more guidance. For his own birthday, his first thought will be how his party can be the most fun for his friends. Like Jed in the story above, Spender kids can get an idea in their heads and have a hard time letting go of it, especially if it's taken off the table because of money. So start talking about expectations a few months before his party. Give him a sense of your budget and have him help you come up with great ideas that don't leave you broke.

When he needs to buy a gift for a friend's party, give him a spending limit and encourage him to get creative about how he uses it. Most kids don't expect extravagant gifts from their peers, so even something as inexpensive as a deck of baseball cards or a collectible figurine can be a great gift that doesn't cost a lot.

Risk Taker

 Risk Takers can get a little, well, imaginative when it comes to birthday parties—rock climbing, rafting, laser tag, or clay pot painting. Some ideas might work well for you, but be ready for other requests that are hard to get out of their minds.

Thankfully, Risk Takers don't feel the need to spend a lot of money to have an adventure-rich birthday. If you have a budget in mind, talk to your Risk Taker about it and have her come up with her top five ideas for celebrating within those limits. She'll love the adventure of planning a great party and figuring out how to have fun without spending much.

When giving gifts to your Risk Taker, focus on experiences instead of material goods. A day of kayaking with you or a series of ski lessons will be far more meaningful for your Risk Taker than another toy or video game. Not only will this kind of gift speak to your child's Money Personality, it will give you a chance to spend time with your fun, adventuresome Risk Taker.

Security Seeker

 If you want to give your Security Seeker a great birthday gift, plan his party three months ahead of time. Okay, not really, but your Security Seeker will indeed want to know what the plans are and that they aren't going to change.

As you put a party together, keep your Security Seeker in the loop as much as possible. Being involved with the details will keep him from getting anxious as the party gets closer. You'll also find that having a hand in the plans means your child won't really care how extravagant or expensive the party is. What matters most to him is that he feels good about the plans and can see it all coming together.

Holidays need a similar approach. Security Seekers do well making a wish list for gifts so they have some control over what they get. If that seems as though it takes the wonder out of the holiday, keep in mind that Security Seekers have pretty clear ideas about what they like—these are kids who dig in deep to a hobby or a collectible game, and they won't get tired of gifts that feed their interests. They truly enjoy getting what they asked for. They don't need surprises and they don't need variety. It might not be exciting to you, but it will be just right for your Security Seeker.

Flyer

 Flyer kids want nothing more than to be with their friends. That makes birthday parties a breeze! Your Flyer won't be all that concerned about the details of the party as long as she knows her friends will have a great time. Get her thinking about ways to make the most of her time with her friends—some party plans lend themselves better to connecting than others. Focus on group games and activities rather than individual competitions or places where kids can run around on their own.

When it comes to gifts, your Flyer is going to love anything that builds up her relationships, so focus on finding games you can play as a family or signing her up for activities she can do with a friend. And use gift-giving opportunities like holidays and birthdays to introduce your Flyer to some basic money concepts, like working within a budget. Because these lessons will happen in the context of getting a gift for someone she cares about, your Flyer will be more tuned in to these lessons than she would be during some random conversation at the grocery store or the kitchen table.

Button Pushers for Parents

Holidays and birthdays are supposed to be great times to celebrate friends and family. But boy can they be stressful! Pay attention to your own Money Personality triggers to make sure you can get through family gatherings, birthday parties, and all the shopping and spending they involve with your sanity intact.

Saver

When we talk to Savers, they almost always tell us that two of their least favorite things are shopping for Christmas gifts and planning birthday parties. Since we're both Spenders, we didn't understand at first what the problem was. But the more we've dug into what makes a Saver tick, the clearer it has become. Both of these—holidays and birthdays—are a slow, steady drip of money coming out of the bank. It's one thing to have one big expense now and then. But holidays and birthday parties can nickel-and-dime Savers until they reach the limits of their sanity.

The best way for you to avoid that feeling of being picked apart one cupcake at a time is to set a clear budget for these occasions. And don't automatically say no to a destination birthday party. Often, places that cater to kids' parties will include pizza and drinks, decorations, and entertainment. In some cases, it can actually be cheaper to hold the party off-site instead of buying all those things and hosting the party at home. So know what you can spend, keep your options open, and watch your stress decrease.

Spender

 One of the hardest parts of being a Spender is knowing when to pull back on spending for the sake of other people. This is one of those areas where Spenders have to be very careful not to equate spending money with showing love.

It's okay to say no to our kids' requests for elaborate parties and expensive gifts. They might not like it, but modeling restraint in our spending can actually be a great gift to our kids. They will be adults one day, and it's essential that they learn that money isn't the answer to everything. They need to see that they can be happy and get the things they really need in life without spending a ton of money or having someone give them everything they want. That lesson needs to start with you.

Risk Taker

Risk Takers can make any occasion more fun, but keep your child's comfort level in mind as you make plans for birthday parties and holiday celebrations. What might seem awesome and memorable to you could just be too much action or adventure for your child or her friends.

You can still bring your spirit of fun to the party, however. As you plan with your child, get her thinking about unique or interesting ways to celebrate. Instead of the same old Party Zone birthday, why not collect cardboard boxes and use the time to build an epic fort in your backyard? Or take the kids on a scavenger hunt through a cool nature preserve in your area. Grand adventures don't have to cost much.

Security Seeker

As tempting as it is to plan a birthday party or holiday gathering on your own, it kind of defeats the purpose. You might have a nice, tidy plan, but you'll have alienated the very people you want to celebrate.

Resist the urge to have a master plan, and find a way to be comfortable with a little bit of wiggle room. It's always a good idea to know roughly what you can afford to spend on a party, on gifts, on a holiday feast, but don't let money and a need for control get in the way of experiencing the fun of an eight-year-old's birthday or the joy of opening presents on

Christmas morning. Trust that even if the plan falls apart a bit, you have the skills to recover and readjust.

Flyer

Flyers love a good party, and birthday parties are no exception. But Flyers can also get so caught up in creating the perfect event that they lose sight of the real purpose of the gathering— to celebrate.

Before you get carried away with all the dreams you have for giving your child the best party ever, check in with him to make sure he's on board with your ideas. And check in with your budget too. Flyers can quickly overspend in an effort to put together an incredible event. But even the most magical birthday party won't make up for a blown budget down the road. Do your best to pay attention to the money side of your decisions and trust that the fun will take care of itself.

9

Dealing with Relatives

It is Hope's ninth birthday, and the whole family is gathered to celebrate. When Hope was a baby, she went through several surgeries for a heart defect. Now a happy, healthy third grader, Hope shows no signs that her life had once been so fragile. But her family certainly remembers how scary those early years were, and every birthday is a cause for serious celebration.

Both sets of Hope's grandparents have come to town for this special family birthday party. Her maternal grandparents are from a small farming community a few hours away. Her dad's parents have flown in from their winter home in Arizona. While the four grandparents always get along just fine, Hope's parents notice there is often an undertone of competition between them: Who gets to see more of the grandkids? Who knows more about them? Who can get them the most beloved gift? Predicting the one-upmanship this birthday party might provoke, Hope's mom and dad each asked their respective parents to forgo a big gift and instead donate that money to a charity that helps pay for heart surgeries for children in Haiti.

Hope is all for this idea. When she had her birthday party with her friends, she asked them to skip the gifts and instead contribute to this same charity if they wanted to. Together, she and her friends were able to send almost $200 to the organization, which made Hope very proud.

When it comes time to open gifts, Hope knows she will have a few small gifts, but she is surprised to see a beautifully wrapped gift sitting by the couch. She opens it and finds a brand-new iPad in a hot pink case, a gift from her paternal grandparents. Not to be outdone, her maternal grandmother pulls a small box out of her purse and hands it to Hope. Inside is a small pair of diamond studs. "Every girl should have a pair of diamond earrings," she says as Hope looks at the sparkly jewels in front of her.

"Um, thank you, everyone," Hope says as she hugs her family and heads into the kitchen for more cake.

Hope's parents are livid. They had been so clear with their parents, and their request has been completely ignored. On top of that, they have ignored what Hope wanted. Of course she is thrilled with the iPad and the earrings—what kid wouldn't be?—but she had wanted to do something more meaningful, and that got pushed aside in the name of some ridiculous bid for affection. What started out as a lovely day slowly dissolves into a tense afternoon. Hope's mom can barely look at her in-laws. Hope's dad tries to brush it off, but he is frustrated with the family too.

Neither of them wants to ruin the day with a confrontation, so they let it go; but as they clean up later that night, they wonder if they will ever get through to their parents.

As we thought about the money conversations that are most important at this stage of a child's life, we kept coming back to this issue of gifts from family members. We knew we needed to address this conflict, but we couldn't figure out how to come at it from a Money Personality angle. And that's when it occurred to us: it's not Hope's Money Personality we need to talk about; it's Grandma's.

So we're going to shift gears for this chapter. Instead of thinking about your child's Money Personalities, we want you to think about the Money Personalities you see in your children's grandparents and other family members who regularly give gifts to your children. Go back to chapter 2 for a minute and look over the descriptions of the five Money Personalities. Figure out which ones seem to best fit your parents, in-laws, and siblings. You don't have to be 100 percent certain about your guesses. You just need a general sense of how these other adults in your children's lives think about and deal with money. Having a better understanding of how Grandma and Grandpa (or Aunt Sarah and Uncle Pete or whoever) think about money will help you address potential conflict in a far more productive way than just trying to stop the flow of cash and prizes.

There are all kinds of reasons something as simple as gift giving can trigger a family argument. We find that most parental concerns fall into one of three categories:

- Fear of spoiling the kids
- Inappropriate gifts
- Ignoring requests

The first is pretty obvious. We live in an age of indulgence. It seems as though every kid in America has his own phone, her own iPod, designer clothes, the latest cool shoes. Kids want, and they seem to get. But so many parents are trying to stem the influx of stuff. Sometimes it's for economic reasons, but even families that can afford to give their children anything they ask for hold back because they want to instill lessons about hard work and rewards and contentment and generosity. So when grandparents or aunts and uncles come along and indulge our kids, it feels as if they are undoing the lessons we're trying to teach.

Then there's the issue of inappropriate gifts. Whether it's Uncle Jack giving little Mandy a drum set for Christmas or Grandpa giving your six-year-old a gun for his birthday, there are some gifts you wish had never crossed the threshold of your house. And once they are in, it's very hard to get them back out. Sometimes it's not the gift itself that's problematic but the amount of money that has been spent—does an eight-year-old really need her own laptop? You know the intentions are good, but the gift is just not the right fit for your family.

Finally, there are those situations like the one Hope's parents dealt with—a request that gets ignored. We know families who have asked grandparents to limit their Christmas gift giving to one or two items per child, only to be met with a toy-store explosion on Christmas morning. Other parents set boundaries based on their family values—no violent video games, only certain movies or music—and find that Aunt Samantha has decided she doesn't care. In these situations, parents feel a lack of respect from their relatives, something that can put a dent in any holiday celebration.

These are all legitimate concerns, and in theory, it should be fairly easy to address them. But the gift-giving conflicts are tangled up with a desire to be grateful, to recognize that grandparents and aunts and uncles are showing love for the kids through these purchases. It's not easy to tell Grandma to back off on the gifts when it's one of the main ways she has of connecting with her grandchildren. But when you have a better understanding of your relatives' Money Personalities, you can start to dig into the reasons they give the way they do and hopefully find some compromises that help everyone get what they want.

Here's how to talk about gift giving with your child's relatives if they are:

Savers

 While many families struggle to rein in overspending grandparents, you will find yourself facing a different set of issues. Savers can come across as cheap on holidays, because they either will not give a gift at all or will give something generic they got on sale. Okay, that's a bit of a stereotype, but if you have a Saver grandparent, you know it's not too far off the mark.

Here's the thing: you are never going to get a Saver to become a Spender. So consider letting your Saver off the hook when it comes to gifts. Savers often give gifts at birthdays and holidays out of obligation. But they have lots of other ways of showing their love and care for the people in their lives. So suggest to your Saver that they gift your kids with experiences instead of stuff. Maybe they would like to take the kids to the zoo or gift your family with a membership to a science museum. Savers have a hard time spending money on things they perceive as unnecessary, but spending on experiences is worth every penny, even to the staunchest Saver.

Spenders

 Asking a Spender to stop spending is like asking them to stop loving your kids. They can't, and your request will only lead to hurt feelings.

At the same time, you're dealing with grownups who can handle a calm, rational conversation about your concerns. If you feel as if your Spender relatives are ignoring your requests to pull back, talk about your fears of your children being spoiled or coming to expect lavish gifts. Then work together to find some middle ground.

We talked to one couple who did just that with a set of Spender grandparents. Instead of buying multiple gifts for the grandkids, they now split their gift giving: they give a more modest gift and contribute another chunk of money to their grandchildren's college funds. This has been a win-win for this family. Grandma and Grandpa get to shower their grandkids with gifts and help set up a more secure future for them. The kids get nice gifts, but not so many that they forget to appreciate them. And Mom and Dad are getting some financial help for college.

As you talk with the Spenders in your extended family, be careful not to sound ungracious. Giving gifts is a huge part of how Spenders show their love for people, and you don't want to risk hurting their feelings or making them feel their expressions of love are unwelcome. So frame this conversation in relationship terms. Remind them that the kids love them no matter how many gifts pile up at the birthday party.

Risk Takers

 Because Risk Takers love adventure, they are more likely to give inappropriate gifts than other Money Personalities. They're not clueless; they just want to see the people they love enjoy life. So they will buy a supercool bike that's two sizes too big for the child. Or buy a zip line for your backyard, even though your kids are too short to reach it. The Risk Taker is all about having a blast, and she's going to make sure your kids are having one too.

Because of their love of adventure, Risk Takers don't always see the practical side of gifts. So you can help them choose a little more carefully by keeping them clued in to your child's interests, his wish list, even his clothing size. Your bachelor brother you only see at holidays probably has no idea a six-year-old is still getting used to riding a bike and can't really handle a unicycle just yet. So give him some parameters and trust that he will give something a little more age appropriate.

At the same time, having a Risk Taker in her life can itself be a great gift for your child. That relative is likely to introduce her to some amazing experiences. It might be her Risk Taker grandma who takes her on her first airplane ride. It might be that Risk Taker uncle who takes her kayaking or deep-sea fishing or hiking through the Rockies. These invaluable experiences are a great way for a Risk Taker to add adventure to your child's life.

Security Seekers

The challenge with Security Seekers won't necessarily be with the Security Seekers themselves. It will be your kids who might need some coaching in this relationship.

Security Seekers are often great gift-givers. They know how to plan and create airtight budgets. But they always have an eye on the future. So the gifts they tend to give are likely to have a sense of predictability and safety about them. Your kids might even find them boring. We heard about a Security Seeker who gave her teenage grandson her collection of vintage Fiestaware for Christmas. Can you imagine the look on this kid's face when he opened a huge box only to find bright blue plates? What he didn't know was that that box of plates—and cups and saucers and pitchers and serving platters—was worth a ton of money, enough to pay a good chunk of his college expenses if he chose to sell it.

If you find that the Security Seeker in your family tends to give practical gifts or gifts aimed at making your child's future a little more comfortable—a savings bond, a few shares of a low-risk stock, a family heirloom—prepare your kids ahead of time. Help them see the love behind these unflashy gifts, and remind them to be thankful and gracious even if they don't feel that immediate rush that comes from a new video game or sports equipment.

Flyers

 Flyer grandparents, aunts, and uncles can be a little hard to talk to about gift giving. They are so tuned in to building relationships with your children that they can take any requests or limits from you as you interfering in their connection with the kids. So be patient and decide when, how, and if you really need to have this conversation.

The Flyer's approach to gift giving will often come from her Secondary Money Personality, so keep that in mind as you talk through any concerns. But as you do, emphasize how much you value the relationship the Flyer has with your family. Do everything you can to keep the focus on your reasons for asking for a change. The Flyer wants to protect her relationship with you as well, so when she sees you working to keep that relationship strong, she'll do her part to work with you.

Button Pushers for Parents

The way you react to the gifts given by grandparents and other extended family members has as much to do with your Money Personalities as it does with theirs. Knowing your own emotional triggers will help you predict and prepare for gift-giving events.

Saver

So many Savers we know have a love/hate relationship with holidays and birthdays, because they have such a hard time both giving and accepting gifts. For Savers, it's hard to turn off that part of their brains that thinks about how much something costs, especially when that something is for your kids. So you might find that you sit around the Christmas tree and think about how much money people wasted on useless gifts instead of seeing the joy those gifts can bring.

Do your best to put that voice to bed on holidays. When someone gives your child a gift, dig deep and try not to think about the money. Focus on the love, the thought, the care that someone put into choosing that item. Think about the joy it's bringing your child. Even if you think it's useless, it's a symbol of affection from someone who loves your kids. Let that be enough.

Spender

It's hard for Spenders to sit back and enjoy watching other people receive gifts, and it's not because they wish they were getting the gifts. It's because Spenders can be very judgmental when it comes to gifts. We Spenders like to give the very best we can—even if we can't always afford it—and when we see other people give gifts we think are cheap or poorly made or not very well thought out, we can feel a little superior.

So watch out for that pride. Remember, not everyone gets a rush from shopping the way you do. Not everyone can afford or feels comfortable spending a ton of money on gifts, especially gifts for children, who are notoriously fickle in their taste in toys and games and everything else. Be gracious, say thank you, and acknowledge the kindness at the heart of that gift. Keep your judgments to yourself.

Risk Taker

 Your mother might give your child a hand-knit sweater for Christmas every year. And that will drive you crazy. You want to see your kids experience life. You want them to get gifts that fuel their imaginations and spark new ideas. You want them to get sporting gear and tickets to the theater and tap dancing lessons. And instead they get sweaters.

Keep in mind that bringing a sense of adventure into your child's life doesn't have to come from out-there experiences and supercool gifts. For kids, life is a pretty great adventure just the way it is. Help them celebrate the joy that comes from being with family, from building relationships, from celebrating together. There will always be opportunities for excitement. There won't always be sweaters from Grandma. Do your best to stay grounded in the present and see the adventure that's right in front of you.

Security Seeker

 For Security Seekers, the best gifts are useful gifts. The more practical the gift, the better. But not everyone sees gift giving in that light. Some people like to give gifts that are all about fun or indulgence, especially to kids. Your challenge is to avoid imposing your ideas about what makes a worthy gift on other people.

Security Seekers can be so focused on accomplishing goals, especially those with a money component—paying for college, saving for a car—that they can lose sight of enjoying the moment. Children, of course, are all about the moment, and many of the people in your life who give gifts to your children will be playing into your child's here-and-now mentality. So they might buy gifts that will break quickly. They might buy gifts your child will get tired of by next week. They might buy trendy toys or games or gadgets. And that's going to be hard for you to take. So prepare yourself for this inevitable internal conflict and decide ahead of time that you're not going to be the voice of reason this year. If the worst thing that happens is that your child gets a silly toy that breaks in a day, that's a pretty great holiday.

Flyer

 Flyers don't have many buttons that get pushed when their kids get gifts from relatives. You aren't thinking about how much gifts cost or whether they are worth the money. But you will have one hot button: fairness.

Flyers hate to see people get their feelings hurt, especially their kids. So if you perceive that one child is getting more or better or cooler gifts than another, you'll find yourself starting to overcompensate for it. You'll spend more time with that child or maybe re-tag some gifts to even things out. But be careful about projecting your sense of fairness on the situation. If one of your children is feeling genuinely left out or cheated, pull her aside for a conversation about those feelings. But kids don't always see these situations the way adults do. One child's precious doll can, in her mind, outweigh her brother's pile of video games. So keep your concerns to yourself unless you see a real need to intervene. Even then, don't assume anything about your family members' motives. Keep those relationships strong too.

10

Money Personality Goals for Ages 5-12

While every person has a combination of two Money Personalities, a combination that can't be changed, it is essential that we help our kids expand their skills beyond their Money Personalities. Every Spender needs to learn how to save. Every Security Seeker needs to learn when to let go a little bit. Building a few skills outside of their Money Personalities will help your children have a more well-rounded approach to money in general.

Goals for Savers

 Savers can get stuck saving money out of habit rather than thinking about money as a means to an end. To make sure your child is learning to save with a purpose, help him establish a few short-term and long-term (no more than a year away for this age group) goals for his savings. These don't have to be major purchases, but having a plan helps keep your child from getting obsessive about the money itself.

To help your child balance his Saver Money Personality, find ways to help him flex his Spender, Risk Taker, and Flyer muscles. Find a charity or fund-raising cause your child can get excited about—schools, churches, and camps often have short-term fund-raisers going on that your child can take part in with both his money and his time. This kind of contribution develops a spirit of generosity in children and reminds them that their money and talents can be powerful tools for doing good in the world. Remember, kids at this age want to feel as though they can impact the world around them. Charitable giving is a great way to help them do just that.

Goals for Spenders

Spenders can be generous to a fault, often giving away things that aren't really theirs to give—toys, money, books, clothes. By no means do you want to squelch that instinct to give, but Spenders need to learn when to pull back if they are going to have a balanced perspective on money.

Even if your Spender has access to only a little bit of weekly allowance, start building a saving and spending plan as soon as you can. If your six-year-old gets a dollar a week for her allowance, set up a system like this: Every month she can spend two dollars however she likes, she gives one dollar away to church or a cause she's interested in (at this age that might mean handing the dollar back to you to add to any charitable donations you have), and she saves one dollar for a long-term goal, like a toy or a bike or something else she has had her eye on. You can alter this equation to fit your situation, but we suggest keeping the spend/save/give amounts fairly equal.

It won't be easy to keep your Spender on track; remember that your young Spender doesn't have the ability to think abstractly about the future. She is all about immediate gratification and fun. But with practice and some guidance from you, she'll get the hang of putting off until tomorrow what she really wanted to buy today.

Goals for Risk Takers

 Risk Takers love adventure. And while that can lead to impulsive decisions, it also means that Risk Takers can do a great job of balancing their love of the unknown with concrete plans.

Your Risk Taker probably has lots of big ideas about what he wants to do with his money (and your money!). He wants to start a pet-sitting business or build a go-cart to enter in a race. He wants to plan a bike trip to Montana or spend a week fishing in all five Great Lakes. Whatever his plans are, there's no doubt they will cost money. So get your Risk Taker to think through the details of his plans. What can he do to earn and save some of the money it will take to make these dreams happen?

Once his wheels get turning, help your child stay grounded in the present by giving him the tools to track his savings—an Excel spreadsheet, an old-school ledger, a big jar he dumps his change into—so he can see how close he's getting to his goal. That visual reminder will motivate him to balance his need for adventure with careful planning.

Goals for Security Seekers

 Security Seekers need help balancing their strong planning abilities with a willingness to be spontaneous. When it comes to money decisions, you can guide your Security Seeker toward a little less control by having her join you in planning a future family event. If you have a vacation or even a weekend outing planned, hand over a financial decision or two to your Security Seeker. Encourage her to do a little research, to help make a budget, to figure out just what your family needs to make this event happen.

Once she has it figured out, ask her to help you plan a surprise for the rest of the family. Maybe there's a great place to get ice cream on your way to the zoo. Or maybe you can all take a pottery class while you're on vacation in the mountains. She doesn't have to work out all the details of this surprise, but throwing a fun little curveball into her plans helps her break out of her need to have everything mapped out. She'll see how much fun it can be to try something new.

Goals for Flyers

 Your Flyer is all about relationships, so you're never going to help him think about money unless it's connected to what matters most to him—people. You can help your child build some basic money skills by giving him the simple goal of planning an activity with a couple of friends, something that has a price tag attached. Maybe he wants to get pizza and play laser tag, or go to a movie, or head to the mall for ice cream and arcade games. Give him a basic budget to work with and make a game of helping him figure out how to best spend the money to have a great time with his friends.

Make It Happen!

SECTION 3

· · ·

Ages 13–17

11

Inside the Mind of Your Teenager

Okay, take a deep breath. Just reading the title of this chapter might have you a little nervous—does anyone want to be inside the mind of a teenager? It was bad enough to *have* the mind of a teenager once upon a time. But if you have a teenager in your life, you know that every little bit of information you can get about why that kid acts the way he does can only help.

Jeremy is like most fifteen-year-olds. He can act sweet as can be to his grandmother and outright rude to his mother, sometimes in the same sentence. His parents wonder how he has managed to keep all of his limbs since he always seems to have some sort of injury from racing on his little sister's bike or using the neighbor's trampoline to jump over the backyard fence. He is also creative, funny, and smart, yet seems to lack even the tiniest bit of common sense. He is, in a word, a knucklehead.

Jeremy's parents know that part of his goofiness is just the way teenage boys are. But they worry that as he gets ready to start high school he's lacking the basic discipline he'll need to keep up with the increased homework and sports schedule that's coming. So they've been trying to help him settle down a bit and take more responsibility for his own time and money management. They cut back on his allowance and told him it was time for him to find ways to make his own money. They've given him some additional responsibility for his own schedule, leaving it to him to get himself to baseball practice and arrange for rides to friends' houses. They hope that doing all this will help Jeremy take life a bit more seriously.

But so far, they aren't seeing many results. Instead of getting some kind of part-time job or even mowing lawns in the neighborhood, Jeremy has been borrowing money from friends and taking out "loans" from his younger sister, who hoards her allowance like there has been a run on the bank. And it's not like he spends this money on things he needs. Instead, he does things like hatch a plan with a friend to build their own bikes, only to discover they bought a bunch of tools they really don't know how to use. To his parents, he seems to make these kind of boneheaded decisions about once a week.

That's not to say Jeremy is a bad kid—not at all. He's incredibly talented and artistic. He loves to make short movies with his buddies that never fail to make his parents laugh. He's already talking about heading to film school after he graduates and has all kinds of ideas for movies he wants to make one day. He is a great brother who plans fun adventures for his sister and her friends. He's the life of the party at family gatherings and makes friends with kids and adults alike. He's a leader in his church youth group and is well liked by teachers and students at his school.

Jeremy is indeed a typical teenager—a mess of contradictory behaviors and questionable decision-making skills. Fortunately, Jeremy hasn't gotten himself into any real trouble yet; but like so many teenagers, he's one bad decision away from doing real harm to himself or others. And that's what terrifies his parents.

The teenage brain is a weird little machine. The early years of puberty mark one of the most disruptive periods of brain development in a person's life span, second only to the toddler years. There are new synapses being formed and all kinds of hormones washing over the whole thing, making for a truly turbulent life stage. Until teenagers are through puberty, they really don't have much control over their emotions and decision making.

Even then, the brain is still in the middle of some serious development. New brain research suggests that the brain doesn't finish making all the connections needed for good decision making until somewhere in our midtwenties. That means teenagers are not fully able to think through cause and effect, make predictions about consequences, or think clearly and rationally about relationships or even the future.

For kids like Jeremy, that looks like the kind of dopey, irresponsible behavior that's driving his parents crazy. Add the fact that Jeremy is a Risk Taker/Flyer, and you have a kid who is not going to make clear, rational decisions about money—or anything else—anytime soon.

Teenagers are also doing plenty of emotional work during these years. We all hear a lot about rebellious teenagers, and while it is certainly true that teenagers tend to push hard against parental authority, it's a little unfair to say that this is simple rebellion. Most teenagers are looking for the boundaries of their independence. They aren't trying to break out of the yard as much as they are edging toward the fence to see how far they can go.

That's why teenagers need more parent involvement, not less. Sure, teenagers act as if they want nothing to do with their parents, but most teenagers truly want and need to know what's expected of them as they try to sort out what they expect of themselves. In a lot of ways, this is the stage when you are slowly handing over the controls of your child's life. She certainly isn't ready to fly the airplane all by herself yet, but as she moves through her teen years, she's increasingly looking for opportunities to be your copilot.

This is particularly true when it comes to money decisions. For teenagers, money really does equal freedom. It's not just the Spenders who feel that way. Savers love that sense of control they get when they have full oversight of their finances; it feels like freedom to be the one who decides how that money will be spent—or not spent. Security Seekers want to have a say in what the future looks like, and they feel better having a role in preparing for it. So every money decision your teenager is making is surrounded by her need for more freedom, more input, more responsibility.

This also can be an incredibly challenging time to help your child develop strong money habits, because he is highly likely to make dumb money decisions. You'll need to have a very good understanding of your own Money Personalities to help you avoid arguments based on nothing more than a different perspective on money. And if you and your teenager have opposite Money Personalities, buckle up, because this will be an easy place for your teenager to push your buttons and fight for independence.

Part of what gets to Jeremy's parents is how irresponsible he seems to be about money. So they have tried to clamp down, pushing him to be in charge of his own income. But he's not biting. Why? Because he's a Risk Taker/Flyer. The Risk Taker part of him is looking for fun and adventure; the Flyer is all about relationships. So responsibility, planning, and saving are nowhere close to being on his radar. When his parents talk to him about saving money or getting a job, they might as well be speaking Latin to him. He just doesn't get it. And that's driving his Security Seeker dad and Saver mom out of their minds.

This is a great stage to really focus on the difference between finances and your Money Relationship with your child. Remember, financial details are a different issue than the way you talk about and deal with money. The details of your child's spending are part of a financial conversation. But it's your Money Relationship—the way you communicate about finances, the way you make decisions, the way you work or don't work together on money matters—that is the real focus of these conversations. No matter how your child is spending or saving money, stay tuned in to the relationship you're building with your child. You might disagree with the decisions he makes, but that should never be a reason to let your Money Relationship suffer.

Knowing your own Money Personalities and your child's Money Personalities is central to keeping your Money Relationship solid. We'll move into the specific money conversations you need to have with your teenager starting with the next chapter. But first, we want to lay out a few of the general developmental themes that run through money conversations with teenagers. We'll also suggest goals for helping your teenager find balance in her Money Personalities.

Identity Is the Biggest Question

Who am I going to be? If there's any deep thinking going on in your teenager's brain, it's this question. Every behavior, idea, dream, conversation, relationship, argument, drama, rebellion you see in your teenager is motivated by her need to figure out who she is and who she wants to be. Experts say that these are the years when children try on various identities to find one that fits. So they go through weird goth phases or try out for the school play when they've never set foot on a stage before. They are experimenting with identity.

That's probably not news to you, but it's an important reminder as we parents try to guide our children into good money habits. They aren't always going to act in consistent ways. Your Saver might go off on a spending spree because all of his friends have the latest game system and he wants to fit in. Your Risk Taker might decide she wants to go to college in Paris and suddenly start saving money with a single-mindedness you never imagined she had.

When teenagers act erratically, they need their parents to withhold immediate judgment and measure their reactions—your teenager is already supersensitive about making mistakes and messing up. Her efforts to figure out who she is are fraught with missteps, and she is deeply afraid of being seen as stupid or a failure or—worst of all—a child. So instead, talk to your teenager as calmly as you can about her decision. What is she hoping to gain from it? How does she feel about the way things are playing out? You might be surprised at your teenager's ability to see problems in her decisions even without you bringing them up.

When you notice your teenager making good decisions about money or anything else, tell her. Let her know that you noticed. She might act all embarrassed, but deep down, she'll appreciate you seeing the good in her at a time in her life when she can get preoccupied with the ways she doesn't measure up.

Freedom Now!

Again, the idea that your teenager craves more freedom is probably not news to you. But you might find yourself surprised at how deeply this current runs through your child's money decisions.

The tricky thing for parents during this stage is to step back and let our kids make money mistakes. For the most part, there's nothing major at stake, unless you've put your fourteen-year-old in charge of your retirement account—which you really shouldn't do. But giving your teenager little bits of financial freedom now is going to have big payoffs down the road. A teenager who spends all his money on a hipster bike that falls apart after one summer is going to remember that lesson for a long time. In the same vein, a teenager who sets up a savings goal for himself, even if it's something you think is a waste of money, is going to work harder to get money in that account than a kid whose parents decide what he should do with his money.

That doesn't mean you have to let your teenager have his way all the time. But as you slowly give him more control over his own finances, set up explicitly clear expectations about any savings or charitable giving you want to see, and give him the tools to track his income and outgo. If he blows it, talk through what went wrong and help him figure out ways to avoid the same problems in the future. This mix of freedom and responsibility is exactly what your teenager wants and needs right now.

The Future Is Looming

If you think you're freaking out about your child graduating and leaving home, well, you're not the only one. Believe it or not, your teenager is at least as nervous about her future as you are—maybe even more. While she might not be thinking about the financial piece the way you do, she is still looking at the next stage of life and seeing a huge, gaping hole called the unknown. And it's scary.

As you and your teenager start thinking about and planning for the future, keep in mind that every conversation about what's coming has a lot of emotional baggage attached to it. If she gets defensive or seems to ignore you when you want to talk about applying for college scholarships, it's not because she's not interested. It's because she's terrified. Or she might be obsessed with saving money and starting to worry that she won't have enough to attend her top-choice school.

To minimize the tension, keep money conversations about the future short and sweet. If there are details to work out, involve your teenager only if she seems interested. If not, don't throw more anxiety on her—she simply can't deal with it, and it will only lead to more conflict. And the more you can keep your own emotions out of these conversations—even if you're more anxious than she is—the better.

12

Discretionary Income

Amber is thrilled when she lands a lifeguard job. At least four of her buddies from the swim team will be working at the same pool, and she knows this is going to be the best summer ever! Not only will she be working with her friends, getting an awesome tan, teaching little kids how to swim, and eating nachos for lunch during her shifts, but she is finally going to have some serious spending money—$72 a week can buy a lot of cute clothes and pay for a lot of movies, pizza, and even a few trips to the big amusement park in town.

When Amber comes home with her first paycheck, she shows it to her parents, who are just as excited as she is about this new financial freedom. "Honey, this is great!" her dad says. "Let's bring this baby down to the bank and get you going with a savings account of your own."

"Um, what?" replies Amber.

"A savings account, honey. You need someplace to deposit this money."

"But I don't really need a savings account. I'm just going to cash the check."

"Um, what?" replies Amber's dad.

What follows is a long and unpleasant conversation about what, exactly, Amber is going to do with her new income. It turns out that she and her parents have veeeerrry different ideas about Amber's financial freedom.

Amber, like most teenagers who are getting an allowance or earning their first paycheck, assumes that if she is the one making the money, then she gets to make all the decisions about spending the money. Her parents, like most parents of teenagers, assume that she will be on board with their plans for her to save some of that money for the future, maybe donate some to her church or another charitable organization, and have a little money left to spend. So it's no surprise that these assumptions crash into each other in the face of that first big paycheck.

After this first conversation breaks down into a door-slamming impasse, Amber's parents know they need to back up and try a new approach with her. But they have no idea how to do that. Amber has always been an independent child—a true firstborn with a strong sense of herself and no lack of confidence. She has never liked being told what to do—a trait that has only gotten stronger during her teen years.

They have encouraged her to get a job so she can have the responsibility of making and keeping track of her own money. She has gotten a small allowance for years, but it is never more than a few dollars a week to use as spending money. But they always find themselves handing Amber a few more dollars for a movie or a new outfit. They like the idea of letting Amber pay for her own entertainment and wardrobe while still learning to save money for the future.

But Amber is a Spender/Risk Taker, and she doesn't want to think about the future, at least not in any realistic way. She would rather enjoy herself right now, when she has fun friends and money in her pocket. When she does think about what's next in her life, it's in totally abstract terms— she wants to live in California and work as a lifeguard while she goes to college. How that will all work out doesn't concern her right now; it just sounds cool.

Amber's parents are at a loss. They want Amber to have some say in how she spends her money—that's an important part of the financial lessons they want her to learn. But they also want her to start saving a little, just to build that discipline into her life. And they would love to see her contribute some money to a charity or cause that means something to her so she'll learn the joy of giving to others. At the same time, they like the idea of not having to shell out more money every time she needs something. They wonder if it's really such a bad idea to let her spend her money the way she wants to.

This is the stage when many kids have their first encounter with disposable income from a job or a bigger allowance. And since money translates to freedom for independence-minded teenagers, there is a lot of emotion behind conversations about money, especially money your teen might think of as "his." Each Money Personality has its own challenges when it comes to working through these conversations.

Here's how to talk about disposable income if your child is a:

Saver

Saver teenagers aren't going to blow their pay-checks on something silly. They aren't going to take their money and head straight to the mall. In fact, most Saver kids will stash their cash in a drawer or deposit that check and never think about what they might do with the money. They're just happy to know it's safe and sound somewhere.

So the challenge with Savers is to help them get comfortable with spending some of their money and even giving some of it away. Savers can harbor a lot of anxiety about spending—they worry that there's a rainy day just around the corner, and they want to be ready for it. As a result, they might forgo some of the fun and adventure of being a teenager—shopping with friends, going out for burgers after a game, going bowling on a Saturday afternoon. They need your help to get over that anxiety hump and learn to spend a little.

If you're not a Saver, it might seem weird to you that spending money is a skill you need to teach your child. But for Savers, spending just doesn't come naturally. Rather than force your Saver to be someone she's not, help her learn to spend and give in ways that make sense to her.

Savers love a deal. So if your Saver is reluctant to spend her money on clothes, point her toward the clearance rack or take her to a vintage store. If she's saying no to invitations from friends because she doesn't want to pay for pizza or ice cream, have her do the research to find a place that has dollar burgers or two-for-one deals. Help her see that she can buy the things she needs and wants without going broke.

Spender

Here's an important equation to remember: Spender + developing decision-making skills = trouble. If your teenager is a Spender, you have your work cut out for you when it comes to helping him make good choices about his disposable income. Spenders tend to be very easygoing about their spending habits, which can be a real asset as they get older and have to spend larger amounts of money on things like cars and housing—it won't freak them out like it will a Saver. But that easygoing attitude can also be a challenge for a Spender when it comes to discretionary income. He won't think twice about spending money, even when he doesn't have much to spend. Your Spender is likely to be out of money before his paycheck clears the bank. Add in the lack of impulse control common in teenagers and you have a kid who will need a lot of structure to help him learn spending skills.

Your Spender will need your help laying out a concrete, realistic plan for spending, saving, and giving money. While we usually suggest an even three-way split between these three things, you might want to consider having a little wiggle room in the "spending" category for this child. Expect that he's going to blow his paycheck the day he gets it until he gets the hang of divvying it up. And be patient, especially if you're not a Spender. It will take time and maturity for your teenager to develop the discipline and decision-making skills needed for good money management. It will also take extra patience on your part. Be careful not to shame your Spender with accusations about carelessness or irresponsibility. Instead, help him think about spending and saving for himself with questions like, "What's something you'd like to save for?" and "How much do you think you could save every month and still have some spending money?" Putting these decisions in his hands—and checking in to see how he's following through with his decisions—gives him some control over his spending but also helps him develop a savings habit that could keep him out of deep debt down the line.

One other note—more than most of the other Money Personalities, your Spender is the kid most likely to give the "But it's my money!" argument. Spenders don't like feeling controlled, and teenage Spenders *really* don't like it. If you're okay with your child doing what she likes with her allowance or paycheck, that's fine. But if you find yourself bristling at this pushback from your teenager, it really is okay to lay out the "While you're living under my roof" argument in return. Explain to your child that there's no "my" money in a family. After all, you spend "your" money to house and feed and clothe the whole family. As the parent, you absolutely get to have some say-so in what your child does with the money she earns if that's what you want to do.

Risk Taker

Risk Takers are all about adventure. You can use that to your advantage as you help your teenager manage her disposable income. Because Risk Takers are always thinking about what's next, they are more inclined to rein in their spending now if it means a great payoff later.

So encourage your Risk Taker to think about the future as she makes plans for her disposable income. Maybe she wants to go to Spain with her high school Spanish class—that's a savings goal that will keep her motivated. Or maybe she wants to set up an Etsy shop online to sell her handmade jewelry. Help her lay out a plan to make it happen and watch how disciplined she can be with her money.

And keep an eye on her spending. Risk Takers can be vulnerable to the crazy schemes teenagers are known for. Your Risk Taker might have a tidy plan to spend, save, and give, only to throw all of those plans out the window when she and her friends decide to start a band. So have a plan in place in which any purchase over a certain amount has to be run by you. She might not think about the fact that her new passion for garage punk means saying good-bye to that trip to Spain. She needs your help to balance her need for an instant thrill with her long-term plans.

Security Seeker

Most teenagers wrestle with some anxiety about the future, especially as they get into the last few years of high school. But Security Seekers can be derailed by this anxiety. You'll notice this stress coming out in the way your Security Seeker manages his disposable income.

You might find that your Security Seeker is starting to obsess about saving for college or a first car, putting the bulk of his income into a savings account or maybe even a low-interest CD instead of spending some, saving some, and giving some. It's great for your teenager to have plans for the future, but not at the expense of enjoying the present. Believe it or not, you might need to encourage your Security Seeker to spend money, especially if his other Money Personality is a Saver.

You'll also need to watch out for buyer's remorse—that icky feeling Security Seekers get after they've spent more than they think they should have. When it comes along, help your child think about the reality of his spending, not his fears. So maybe he spent too much on those tennis shoes. Remind him that it's not the end of the world and that he has the skills to make up for that spending by cutting back a bit on other expenses.

Finally, help your Security Seeker think about the future in concrete terms. Many Security Seekers fear a future that's not likely to come—for your teenager it might be a fear that he won't be able to pay for college or that he'll never be able to afford a car or an apartment. Encourage him to do some research, both online and through conversations with a school guidance counselor, to help him get a more realistic idea about what kind of money he'll need for school and the financial aid options that will be there for him. Or have him browse Craigslist to get an idea of how much a used car really costs. When he starts working with real numbers, not vague fears, your Security Seeker can make money plans that will help him feel more settled about the future while still enjoying the present.

Flyer

 When it comes to managing their disposable income, teenage Flyers need a lot of guidance from the adults in their lives. They need someone to remind them to deposit their paychecks. They need someone to help them think about how much cash they want to have on hand for the week. They need someone to show them how to balance a checkbook and help them decide how much is too much to spend on headphones and remind them that they aren't getting paid for another two weeks.

This might sound like a lot of work for you—and it is—but remember that your Flyer is all about relationships. So think of these lessons and reminders as a way of strengthening your relationship with your teenager. Find ways to make these conversations fun—maybe you can go out for coffee together to plan a budget. Keep pointing out the relational benefits of making good money decisions. If she's smart about saving money, she can use some of it to go on the summer work trip with her youth group. If she avoids spending money on things that don't matter to her, she'll have more to spend when her friends want to head to the mall.

As she develops the skills she needs to make good money decisions, be sure to praise her efforts and progress. When she messes up, try not to be too hard on her—these skills really don't come naturally for her, and even the simplest money conversation can be stressful for a Flyer. Instead, talk through what happened and have her think about how to avoid the same problem in the future. Don't let money get in the way of having a good relationship with your Flyer.

Button Pushers for Parents

Financial independence is a big deal to teenagers, so much so that these conversations can quickly become riddled with tension and conflict. You can do your part to diminish potential arguments by understanding your own Money Personalities and being aware of the ways these conversations can push your buttons.

Saver

 Realize that it will drive you crazy when your children spend their allowance or their income, regardless of what they spend it on. You need to go into any money conversation with your teenager knowing that you can't just impose your expectations on your child. But that doesn't mean you need to stand by while he makes lousy choices. Use the skills that come naturally to you—getting a good deal, making a budget, knowing the difference between wants and needs—to help your child develop good habits, no matter what his Money Personality.

Spender

 Spender parents can get frustrated by their non-Spender children when they seem to be too tight with their money. But they can also get frustrated by their Spender children if they think the kids are spending their money on dumb stuff. If you're a Spender, do your best to take your focus off the dollars. Instead, help your child build up the kind of generous spirit Spenders are known for. No matter what your child's Money Personalities, help her find ways to be generous with her money, her time, and her other resources.

Risk Taker

 Your spirit of adventure can be a great boon to your family, but know that if you have a Saver or Security Seeker child, there will be times when the two of you butt heads. Instead of being critical of your teenager's more conservative nature, make an effort to figure out what you can learn from each other. You can help your teenager add a little adventure to his life, and he can help you enjoy the present a bit more.

Security Seeker

Your instinct is to plan, plan, plan. Your teenager's instinct is to avoid, avoid, avoid. Teenagers are already overwhelmed by thoughts of the future, so if you push conversations about college or jobs or life after high school, they are likely to check out or melt down. Instead, do your worrying and planning on your own, and only bring your teenager into the conversation when you can talk easily and realistically about a concrete plan. Be open to her input and ideas, and keep the lines of communication open. Don't let your stress derail your relationship.

Flyer

 The teen years are hard for Flyer parents because of the natural relationship changes that come along as our children grow up. The financial independence teenagers crave can come across to Flyer parents as just one more way their kids are breaking ties and moving on with life. Do your best not to read too much into your teenager's desire to make his own financial decisions—it really is a normal, natural step in his maturing process and not a reflection of his feelings for you. And even though talking about and thinking about money doesn't come naturally for Flyers, do your best to engage your child and teach him the basics—how to balance a checkbook, how to lay out a simple budget, how to set aside a little for saving and spending and giving. These are life skills every teenager needs.

13

Technology:
The Teenage Gimmes

Shane and his parents have finally reached an agreement. Shane can get a smartphone, but with a few conditions: (1) Shane has to have his phone on and with him when he is out with friends—no leaving it in a car, no turning off the ringer, no ignoring their phone calls. (2) He has to check with them before buying any music or apps on the family account, and they have full veto power. (3) He has to hand over his phone to his parents before he goes to bed every night.

For the first few weeks, this arrangement works out great for everyone. Shane loves his phone. He loves being able to connect with his friends anytime, anywhere. He loves having all of his music and games on one device. He loves watching movies in his room and not having to share the TV with his little brothers anymore. And Shane's parents are happy too. They can contact Shane when they need to. They can pick him up from football practice when he is actually finished instead of waiting in the parking lot when practice runs long. And Shane even calls his grandparents on his own.

Then things start to go south. First, the e-mails start—e-mails from the online music service telling Shane's parents that he has made another purchase; e-mails from their service provider, listing the thousands of texts Shane is sending every few weeks. Shane starts getting so glued to his phone that he is checking his texts during dinner. And it is increasingly rare to see him without his headphones popped in his ears, keeping him disengaged from everyone in the house. What had seemed like a way to stay connected with their son is becoming the very thing pulling him away from them.

Teenagers are drawn to technology like bees to flowers. And when you try to separate them, well, the results are about the same too—painful. When it comes to money decisions for this age group, technology might very well be the one thing they care about most. Whether it's phones, gaming systems, computers, or other tech gadgets, these goodies are status symbols for teenagers. Conversations about technology purchases can quickly get heated when teenagers feel as if they are being held back from keeping up with their peers.

You can work your way through these tricky waters by having a good sense of your teen's Money Personalities and keeping your conversations about technology focused on your child's money strengths. And keep in mind that most of what we're talking about here can be applied to other "gimmes" during the teen years—clothes, shoes, room décor, whatever it is your teenager is constantly asking for.

Here's how to talk about technology if your teenager is a:

Saver

Savers can be great advocates for themselves when it comes to spending money on technology. Since Savers hate to spend more than they have to, your Saver teenager will be more than happy to do the research needed to find the right gadget at the right price. You can even enlist your Saver's help in finding the best phone/Internet/cable plans for the household. Bringing your teenager on board in these decisions is a great way to show her how much you appreciate the care she puts into spending money.

Tech gadgets also make great gifts for Savers, who are reluctant to spend money on themselves. A new phone or game—even last year's model—will mean a lot to a teenager who wants to stay connected to his friends without spending his money.

Spender

The biggest challenge when it comes to technology is that it's constantly being updated. That means your Spender's need to have the newest phone, the latest game, the coolest apps is never satisfied—there's always something newer and better coming. Spenders love to be on the front end of a trend. So just when you think you have your teenager all set up with a nice phone, a cool game, or whatever, along comes the next version. Suddenly the "old" one is no good, and you find yourself having the same conversation—and maybe the same argument—you had just a few months ago.

It's essential for parents of Spenders to lay out clear boundaries with their teenagers. Your child's desire for what's new and cool can be overwhelming, and if you don't have a plan in place for dealing with it, you're never going to break the cycle of tech gimmes. So expect that your child is going to keep asking for new stuff and know how you're going to respond.

Work with your Spender to establish a six-month or even one-year budget for tech spending. Figure out what's realistic, both for your family budget and for your teenager's tech needs. Then stick with that plan, no matter what. When your Spender knows that he has had a part in these plans, he is more likely to stick with them. But check in now and then just the same. Make sure he's not buying updates or apps or games that will blow the budget.

Risk Taker

 A true Risk Taker doesn't just want to have the newest gadget. He wants to be the *first* one to have it. And while that's fun for about a week, you'll find that your Risk Taker gets tired of the new toy fast. It won't work the way he hoped it would or it's too slow or it's not as fun as the old version. So he cycles through the thrill of the new purchase and the disappointment of the reality of the limits of technology. It's exhausting!

Like Spenders, Risk Takers need to have clear limits on how much they can spend on technology. But they also need your help being patient. They need you to help slow them down a little, maybe do some research before jumping on the newest game or the latest phone. Help them learn how to buy smarter, not faster. Like everything else in this stage of life, it will take time for your Risk Taker to learn how to be patient and delay gratification a bit. But it's a skill he'll use for the rest of his life.

Security Seeker

 Security Seekers, like Savers, have a complex relationship with technology. Your Security Seeker probably wants a phone or games or a decent computer, but she's not likely to be too concerned about having a certain brand or staying current with the latest and greatest. And that's a great gift to you as parents!

Still, if you find that her computer is too outdated to be truly useful, help her do the research to find one that will last a bit longer and still fit her budget. She has her eye on the future and might see some tech spending as useless. But if you talk about the future benefits of having a better computer that she'll still be using in three years, she'll be more inclined to listen and invest in something that contributes to her future comfort and security.

Flyer

 Flyers love technology because it's the ultimate relationship tool. They can stay connected to their friends 24/7. They can play games with their friends even when they aren't in the same house. They can Skype with friends on the other side of the world. Facebook, Twitter, Vine, Snapchat—thanks to technology, there's no end to the ways Flyers can stay hooked up with their friends.

Thankfully, your Flyer probably won't care about what kind of technology she has, as long as it allows her to do what she wants to do. But she will need your help making sure she doesn't buy updates without knowing it or go over any texting limits you've set up on her phone plan. We suggest having a monthly check-in to look over her phone bill and any other payments for apps or music, and talk through any issues that you might see—for example, too much time texting or too much late-night gaming.

And of course you'll want to make sure she's finding ways to connect with her friends face-to-face as well. For Flyers in particular, it's easy to fill up their days with a constant flow of virtual interactions with friends while missing out on actual face time with the people in their lives. If you see your Flyer spending more time engaging online than off-line, set limits for her usage and help her balance the virtual world with the real one.

Button Pushers for Parents

Technology often turns into a battleground between parents and teenagers, in large part because our kids are far more tuned in to tech than we are. While most of us are content to carry the same phone around for a whole year, our kids can barely fathom the idea. Most adults don't keep up on the endless stream of new games and apps, so it seems as though our kids are begging for the same game we just got them two months ago. All of that builds into a heap of frustration for both parent and teenager. Prep yourself for these conversations knowing that some of these Money Personality buttons might get pushed.

Saver

Conversations about technology can be particularly hard on Saver parents. So much of what your teenager wants will seem completely unnecessary to you. How many games does one kid need? Why can't he use your old laptop? Does she seriously need a new graphing calculator for school? While you don't have to say yes to every request, try to separate out what feels unreasonable because of the cost and what feels unreasonable because it's unfamiliar to you. Do your best to keep your own biases about what's important out of the conversation—there is a huge generation gap between even the most tech-savvy parent and the average teenager. If you need to say no to something based on finances, then do it. But if you find you're saying no or getting irked over a game or a gadget because it doesn't seem necessary to you, try to keep your thoughts to yourself and really listen to your teenager's reasons for wanting it. If you still want to say no, make sure you're able to explain your reasons.

Spender

The challenge for Spenders in these conversations is that there is no conversation. You are as inclined as any teenager to have the newest and coolest phone or tablet or GPS and will go out and get it for your kids or yourself without talking to anyone. And that can mean big trouble for the family budget. If you know you have a tendency to spend when you really shouldn't, talk as a family about boundaries for tech spending. Think of ways to maximize your resources—share a tablet, invest in one great family laptop and another less-expensive laptop for school projects, rent or trade games instead of buying them. Make it a family effort and you'll not only protect your budget but help your kids learn some valuable money-decision skills.

Risk Taker

 Like Spenders, Risk Takers need to take a good look at their own habits while they work to build good habits in their teenagers. If your teenager has seen you jumping on every new tech trend, it's going to be harder for you to explain why he needs to hold back. You might also find yourself getting frustrated at your teenager's carelessness when it comes to keeping track of his phone or taking good care of his devices. As a Risk Taker, you tend to invest in the good stuff, and it can be irritating to see your kids treat their nice gadgets like used socks. Keep in mind that this is more an indication of their general teenager-ness than a true disregard for the stuff they have.

Security Seeker

 Security Seeker parents aren't necessarily thrifty. You might have no problem spending money on a great computer, but it's the add-ons, the glitches, the little nagging updates that get your goat. You want to know that when you've spent big bucks, you've gotten your money's worth and are set for a while. When it comes to your teenager, you might find that you get most irritated by her requests for updates on gear she already has—another game, updated software, a new printer—because you like to make a decision once and not have to revisit it over and over again. So do your best to be patient with your teenager. Ask her to think about what she might need in a phone or a tablet or a game system before you take the financial plunge and help her get what she truly needs the first time.

Flyer

 Flyer parents can be frustrated more by the fact that technology exists than by individual money decisions about technology. Flyers, maybe more than any other Money Personality, are tuned in to the ways technology affects relationships. We know a Flyer mom who got so sick of her kids texting during family meals that she now has a rule that all phones are deposited in a basket in the garage before meals, not to be returned until dinner is over and the kitchen cleaned up. But Flyer parents need to watch out for being pushovers when it comes to their teenagers' tech purchases. Because Flyers don't think about money, they can easily be talked into spending more than they can afford in the name of keeping in touch with their kids or helping their kids connect with friends. If you're a Flyer, never let yourself make a tech purchase for yourself or your kids without a clear budget and a good sense of what you really need.

14

Social Life

Hannah is only fourteen, but she already has a social life even her older sister envies. Hardly a day goes by that Hannah is not hanging out with a friend to do homework at the coffee shop or heading to the playground to meet her buddies for some serious four-square or riding her bike with some girls from the volleyball team. Every Friday night includes a potential sleepover or at least pizza and a movie at someone's house or the mall.

Hannah couldn't be happier, but her parents are starting to wonder how much is too much. Hannah was a little shy in elementary school, and her parents are thrilled to see her blossoming now that she's in middle school. She has nice friends with nice parents, and they always feel good about Hannah's activities. But between driving her to friends' houses and handing over $10 for this and $10 for that, they feel like Hannah's social life has taken over their entire family life—and budget.

Hannah's parents are at a bit of an impasse when it comes

to dealing with this situation. It's not exactly a problem, but they do feel like they need to set some expectations now before Hannah and her friends are able to drive and have a lot more freedom. However, they know they need to tread lightly. At least Hannah's mom knows that. Hannah's dad is already seeing the dollar signs add up, and he's ready to give Hannah a twenty on the first of the month and let her fend for herself.

For teenagers, these years are all about freedom and relationships. And that means their social lives are not about just the activities they're doing. A teenager's social life is a crucial piece of her development. It's through these friendships that she'll learn more about who she is and who she wants to be. She will discover what people like about her and what it means to be a true friend. These can be hard years for teenagers—childhood friendships fade, new friends come into their lives, and the struggle for identity can make even the kindest friend turn selfish and cruel.

So as parents, we have to find that sweet spot between micromanaging the social lives of our teenagers and leaving them to fend for themselves. Somewhere in the middle is that balance of involvement and input that still leaves room for independence and responsibility. Look, when we know just how to get that balance, you'll be the first to know. But what we do know is that, like everything else, there is a money component to a teenager's social life, one that can make this whole balancing act even harder than it already is.

While there are certainly lots of ways for teenagers to have a great time without spending money, there are also lots of ways for teenagers to get into trouble without spending money. That's why parents tend to like those social activities that involve movies and pizza and adult supervision of some sort—even if it's just the barista at the coffee shop. And those activities cost money.

When Hannah asks her parents if she can head to the funky gift boutique with her friends, her parents know that the next request will be for money. The girls want to go to a movie? Money. Pizza? Money. Even upgrading Hannah's bike into a safer, sturdier multigear bike she can use to get around town was a big financial decision. And that list doesn't even factor in the big-ticket items like the school choir field trip, youth group day at the amusement park, and camp. None of these decisions are solely about Hannah's social life. Every one of them includes that ever-present money component.

Here's how to handle conversations about social life if your teenager is a:

Saver

Because of the money component involved in the average teen's social life, Saver kids can sometimes find themselves holding back and eventually getting left out of the active lives of their peers. A Saver's reluctance to spend money, especially when he hadn't planned on spending it, can leave him on the fringes of friend groups who are all about pizza and movies and skate parks.

You can help your Saver teen work through this by encouraging him to set aside some of his allowance for social activities. Ask him to be as realistic and concrete as he can when thinking about how often he will hang out with his friends, the kinds of activities they might do, and how much money he feels comfortable spending each week or month. Help him understand that spending money is a way of staying connected with his friends and enjoying this stage of life.

You can also encourage him to brainstorm and initiate some activities that don't cost anything—bike rides, an afternoon at the beach, a Ping-Pong tournament at your house. When his buddies call him up for yet another trip to the arcade, he can suggest an alternative. What kids really want is to be together, and since money is likely part of the equation for all of them, they will probably be perfectly content to have fun without spending a dime.

Spender

 Your Spender will have no problem finding fun ways to burn through her allowance—and then some—with her friends. And because Spenders are typically generous with their money, she'll probably have no problem treating her friends on those occasions when they show up at the burger place without money.

And that's where you need to keep an eye on things. It's one thing to set a spending limit and help your teenager learn to abide by it. It's another thing to help her avoid being taken advantage of by her friends.

Spenders are always willing to lend a few bucks to a friend. But with teenagers, it's easy for your Spender's friends to assume your child will always be willing to foot the bill—and she probably will! So have an honest conversation about how much she spends when she's out with her friends. Does she find that she's often the one paying for herself and at least one other person? Does she have some friends who never seem to have any money on them and expect her to cover their expenses? Does she feel like she's expected to pay for others? These are signs that her friends have caught on to her willingness to pay for them and have no problem making the most of that tendency. Help her find ways to maintain her generous spirit without becoming her group's sugar mama.

Risk Taker

 Your Risk Taker won't have just a social life. He'll have a social life on steroids—bungee jumping, whitewater rafting, skydiving . . . you name it, he has probably considered it. And as he gets older and he and his friends have more freedom and more disposable income, the opportunities for him to start living out his adventuresome dreams will come fast and furious.

If you try to squelch this need for adventure, you'll only end up pushing your Risk Taker into rebellion. So instead, help him set some fun goals that give him the chance to save up for the big stuff like flying lessons or a backpacking trip while still having a good time with more down-to-earth pursuits like movies and ball games. That way, he can get a taste of the crazy stuff while balancing his spending with a few less-expensive options.

Security Seeker

If you've been feeling like you need to give your Security Seeker teenager a little shove out of the nest, you might be on the right track. Teenage Security Seekers, especially those on the younger end of their teen years, are less inclined to spend time away from the family than their more adventuresome peers. They like to know what to expect in any given situation, and the vague plans teenagers tend to make feed into the Security Seeker's anxieties about the unknown.

You can help your Security Seeker stay close to her friends and even start branching out a bit by helping her plan activities for herself and her friends. Since it's the unknown that really concerns a Security Seeker, a lot of her fears about not having enough money for an activity or not knowing the plans will fall away if she's the one taking care of the details.

Your Security Seeker will also have a natural inclination to put money away for the big-picture parts of her life—clothes, school expenses, and so forth—but she might not think about budgeting for fun. So encourage her to set aside some money she can use for spontaneous fun with her friends. Knowing she has the other stuff covered will help her feel better about spending a few bucks on fun.

Flyer

Your Flyer teenager is going to need a heavy dose of guidance from you on this one, especially if his other Money Personality is a Spender or Risk Taker. Because your Flyer is all about relationships, there is no invitation that he'll turn down, no party he won't want to attend, no quick run to the arcade he'll want to miss. That means he'll spend all of his money—or all of yours.

When your Flyer asks to hang out with friends, make sure you get a good sense of what they'll be doing and how much, if any, money your child will need. Your Flyer might not know the answers to these questions, so give him the responsibility of getting the details of a social activity even before he talks to you about it. This probably sounds fairly obvious to you, but for a kid who is (a) a teenager and not really inclined to think about details, and (b) a Flyer who is rarely thinking about money, these are questions he probably never thinks to ask. All he knows is that a friend wants to hang out, and that's enough for him.

Getting your child to think through his social plans before they happen will help him develop a bit of discernment and discipline about how he spends his time and his money. And that's a skill that will pay off big time as he gets older.

Button Pushers for Parents

You're going to feel as though every conversation with your teenager involves a request for money. And you'll likely be right. But do your best to keep your cool when these requests come, and respond to each one on its own merits.

Saver

 One of the challenges for Savers in general is that they have a tendency to be joy stealers— the Saver's need to keep a lid on spending can come across to others as unnecessarily controlling and robbing others of opportunities for fun. So while you don't need to say yes to every request for pizza money from your teenager, make sure you aren't automatically saying no either. Consider the request, ask your teenager to think about how much she has already spent on social activities during the week, and have a real conversation about whether you—or she—can afford this one. Make your decisions based on the real numbers, not fear or a need to control.

Spender

 Even Spenders can get frustrated when they feel like they've become the family ATM for their teenagers. Even though your inclination is to say yes to your child's requests for money—spending vicariously is almost as much fun as real spending—take care to listen to that little voice that's telling you there need to be some limits. It's right.

Spenders risk raising entitled kids, the ones who think they should always be given everything they ask for. And those kids are in for some rough life lessons down the road. So setting spending limits—giving them a set amount each week for social activities, expecting them to pay for some fun stuff out of their own money—will not only help them in the future but will help you avoid any pent-up resentment for being seen as a cash dispenser.

Risk Taker

 The frustration for a Risk Taker parent will come when your teenager gets into a "fun rut." Teenagers have a funny pattern in which they find a thing they like to do—ride bikes, meet at the beach, go to a particular coffee shop—and that's what they do for fun. For weeks on end. Only that. For a Risk Taker, this kind of repetition is ridiculous. Why would you do the same thing every Friday night when there are so many awesome things out there to do?

But this pattern is just part of your teenager's process of figuring out who she is and what she likes to do. And all of her friends are doing the same thing. So together, they try being kids who ride bikes or kids who hang out at the beach or kids who drink coffee until one or all of them realizes it's not the right fit and they move on to the next thing.

Yes, it's a little odd, and as a Risk Taker, it will take all of your self-control to not push your teenager to switch things up. Let her explore. Let her be in a rut. As long as she's making good relationship and money decisions, just hang back and watch her explore and figure out who she is.

Security Seeker

Spontaneity is not part of the Security Seeker's toolbox. Unfortunately, spontaneity is the hallmark of being a teenager. So you'll need to watch out for the anxiety that comes from the sheer unknown nature of your teenager's social spending.

Your best weapon against that anxiety is to plan for some increased spending during the teen years. Figure out what's reasonable for your teenager to spend—be sure to include him in this discussion so he can help you put together a realistic picture of what he might be doing—and set that money aside each week or month. Then, when your child pops into the kitchen with yet another out-of-nowhere request for movie money, you'll know exactly how to respond.

Flyer

The hot button for Flyer parents is the tendency to push their teenagers into social situations the kids might not be interested in or ready for.

Flyers are so into relationships that they want to nurture their teenagers' relationships too. That can lead to money problems as well as issues between parent and child.

That need to help your teenager connect with friends can translate into a tendency to throw money at his social life—hosting weekend parties at your house that are great for the kids but hard on the budget, handing over enough money for him to treat his friends to pizza, saying yes to every invitation even when you can't afford it. Not only will this damage your bank account but it can actually hurt your child too. Setting him up as the kid whose parents pay for everything puts him in danger of attracting friends for the wrong reasons. Pushing too hard also keeps your child from discovering his own ways of making friends. So back off a little and let your teenager figure out how social he wants to be. Then fund those activities in a way that makes sense for your family budget.

15

Extracurriculars

Zach is an amazing football player. Not only is he big for his age, but he is fast. Really fast. By sixth grade he had middle school and high school coaches watching him. On top of being a great football player, Zach is also strong in track and basketball. His parents just know the college scholarships will start adding up and Zach's future will be in the bag.

Then Zach hits ninth grade. He is doing strength training, running, summer camps, the whole bit, working hard to make varsity in all three of his favorite sports. And his parents, who had once been so gung ho on supporting Zach's dreams, are starting to realize that by the time they pay for the gas to get Zach to all of his practices and games and camps, the fees for his club sports, the uniforms, the equipment, the coaching clinics, and the other endless costs of having a three-sport athlete, they will have spent as much as they will get from at least one of those precious scholarships. And that isn't even taking into account the time on the road, the hotel rooms, and the fast-food meals eaten in the car between practices.

By fall, the whole family is stressed and spread as thin as peanut butter on toast. But Zach's parents want to support their son's dreams, so despite the signs that it is all becoming too much, they dig deep—emotionally and financially—and push forward.

Every parent of an active teenager knows that feeling— the feeling that your family has been swallowed up by a sport or a club or a show choir or a dance team or whatever extracurricular has captured your teenager's interest. Even if it's just one team or one club, the schedule shows no mercy—there seems to be no such thing as a one-season sport anymore. And what if you have more than one teenager involved in activities? Good night! You might as well sell the house and move into the van since you're spending 90 percent of your family time in there anyway.

But it is possible to find some balance. Granted, it takes some real "sticktoitiveness" and commitment. Let's face it; you will have to make some difficult choices. But if you know your child's Money Personalities and can include him in the decision-making process, your whole family can find a way to keep enjoying those extracurriculars that truly add value to your lives without sacrificing your entire family to the system.

Here's how to talk through decisions about extracurriculars if your teenager is a:

Saver

 The good news is that a Saver teenager will be well aware of the costs of her activities. She might even give you that information before she tells you much about the activity itself: "Dad, can I audition for the school musical? We have to pay a $40 activity fee if we get in." The bad news is that your Saver might opt herself out of activities she would really like to do, simply because she has decided they cost too much.

You can help your teenager explore the activities she's interested in guilt-free by taking the weight of the financial decision off her shoulders. Tell her early in the school year that you hope she'll get involved in sports or music or debate or whatever floats her boat. Most schools have some kind of activity fair or sign-up night when parents and students can look over all the options together. Get as much info as you can and have your teenager do some thinking about what looks appealing. If you need to stick to a strict budget, tell her how much you're able to afford and know that the Saver in her will love the challenge of doing the most for the least amount of money.

Spender

 Your Spender will sign up for anything and everything without thinking twice about the expense. That might be fine with you, but if it's not, be clear about your expectations well before an activity begins.

Teenage Spenders are first and foremost teenagers, which means their decision-making skills are still a work in progress. So he'll sign up for an out-of-state band trip, forget to tell you about it until it's a couple of months away, and leave you scrambling to either find the money to pay for it or pull your child out of the trip. Or she'll bring home the slip from the softball team with the list of uniform pieces— shirt, pants, socks, cleats, warm-ups, team shirt—and ask you for a check for $350 so you can buy all of it, even though you never knew she had plans to join the softball team.

So keep the lines of communication open with your Spender. This means more than being available to talk. You're going to have to be intentional about getting conversations about activities started. As each new season approaches, start talking with your teenager about his thoughts. Does he have plans? Does he have interests? Look at your budget together and talk realistically about how much you can afford to spend on any given activity. Keep up with the whole process of signing up, getting the gear and the schedule, and planning out how all of this will fit into your family life, not the other way around.

Risk Taker

 The great thing about a Risk Taker is that she's going to introduce your family to all kinds of new activities. This year it might be the ski team; next year, gymnastics. And that's awesome. But it's not great for the checkbook. Just when you think your Risk Taker has found her activity and you've invested in skis or tennis lessons or whatever she needed last year, she changes her mind and you're back to selling perfectly good equipment on Craigslist.

Tell your Risk Taker how much you're willing to spend each season—the full total including gear or lessons or travel—and then let her put together a collection of activities that fits into the budget. Be clear that she will need to finish what she starts, so she needs to put some real thought into which activities she chooses. And then let her make a plan. Risk Takers aren't necessarily Spenders, so you might find that your Risk Taker plans out a great season and even saves you some money. She might borrow field hockey gear from a friend, put together a carpool to concerts, or help the team find a less expensive practice field. And that will be part of the adventure too.

Security Seeker

 Security Seekers will help you out in this department, because they are likely to stick with what they know. If your Security Seeker has been playing soccer since kindergarten, he's probably not going to try football anytime soon.

That's nice when it comes to planning out your spending for the season. You know what's coming, and there will be few surprises. But try not to let the consistency of your schedule keep you from encouraging your teenager to try something new. Even if it's just playing a new position on an old team, these experiences can help keep your Security Seeker from getting stuck in his comfort zone.

Flyer

If you wonder what extracurriculars your Flyer will choose, just ask her friends. Whatever they're doing, that's where she'll be too. Your Flyer will almost always choose to be with her friends instead of pursuing her own interests. That's not a huge problem, especially when she's younger, unless she seems to be missing out on trying new things.

You might also find that your Flyer's tendency to follow her friends means lots of unexpected expenses for you. Like the Risk Taker who hops from thing to thing, the Flyer who keeps changing her mind can leave you with a basement full of barely used drum sets, ballet shoes, and hockey skates. As your child moves into her high school years, it's appropriate to encourage her to keep exploring her options, while setting a clear budget for how much you're willing to spend.

Button Pushers for Parents

Saver

The hard part of extracurriculars for Savers isn't the initial cost. It's the way the costs keep coming and coming and coming. It seems like there's always another check to write, always another tournament to travel for, always another something to add to the running tally.

No matter how frustrated you get, try to avoid grumbling to your teenager. He's not to blame for the expense of his chosen activity, and the bigger fuss you make in his direction, the less joy he's going to have from this experience that's costing you money. If you need to complain, take your beef to the coach or the booster club—the people who actually have the power to change things.

Prepare yourself for this reality by budgeting more than you think you need to for your teenager's activities. And stay involved in the communication between parents and coaches or advisors. Things do come up in the middle of a season, but if there are continual surprise costs, ask the coach if there are ways to help make parents aware of these costs up front so they know what they're signing up for. But be prepared—you might find yourself acting as the new communications volunteer for the team!

Spender

 Spenders have a rather surprising hot button when it comes to extracurriculars. It's not the trips out of town, the team buttons and T-shirts and decals, and all the other great stuff that comes along with these activities that will get you. It's that you are likely to be the one who picks up the tab for team pizza night, or buys the team jersey for the kid who can't afford one, or offers to pay for more hotel rooms for the tournament.

Spenders love to take care of other people, but when they overdo it or find that others have started to expect them to foot the bill, resentment can start to undermine the Spender's good intentions. So do some self-checks every now and then to make sure you can truly afford your own generosity and that you are giving out of your desire to do so, not a sense of obligation.

Risk Taker

 Your issues with extracurriculars will often be the result of your own boredom with the same old same old. You might be happy to shell out more money for activities if it means you never have to sit through another JV baseball game or eighth-grade band concert. Do your best to avoid pushing your teenager into activities he might not be interested in just to satisfy your need for adventure and variety. Even if you have to force yourself to attend games or concerts or meets you would rather skip, remember that these years are fleeting and you'll be missing those bleacher seats before you know it.

Security Seeker

 Security Seekers are always looking to the future, which is often a great quality. But the flip side of your innate planning ability is that you can find a reason to worry about nearly anything. So even something that might seem innocuous to other parents, like extracurriculars, can become weighed down by your concerns for the future: Will this activity help my child get into college? Is she learning something she can use later in life? What good is this doing for her?

Even if your child is still a young teenager, you might find yourself trying to map out her path to success with private lessons or club sports or whatever you think she'll need in that distant, mysterious future. You'll need to take care that your concern about your teenager's future doesn't get in the way of your child just enjoying sports or art or music or whatever it is she's doing. Let an interest be just that. Expect that her interests will change as she gets older. And remember that while extracurriculars certainly look good on college applications, they are also just a great part of being a teenager.

Flyer

 Flyer parents will find themselves less concerned with the financial price of extracurriculars than with the relational price. Flyer parents miss their busy kids! Be careful not to limit your child's activities out of a need to keep him close to home. The shift from spending time with family to spending time with friends is a natural part of the teen years. As hard as it can be on parents, it's a necessary step in the growing-up process.

But Flyer parents do have some financial buttons that can get pushed here as well, especially if you have a very social child who loves to get involved. Because you value relationships so much, you will be willing to let your teenager join anything and everything in the name of friendship, even when you can't afford it. Make sure you have a good sense of your family budget for activities before the season starts so you know when you can say yes and when you might need to say no.

16

Planning for the Future

Cici can't wait to start eighth grade. She will finally be at the top of the middle school food chain, and she and her friends are going to have the best year ever! They are all going to try out for the volleyball team, even though only a few of them have played before and that was in the rec league. But even if they're terrible, they are going to have a blast. Cici also wants to run for student council, keep playing in the band, and write for the school newspaper. She is pumped!

Cici's parents are glad she's excited about school, and they are certainly happy she wants to be involved in activities. But since Cici turns fourteen this year, her parents think it's time for her to get some kind of starter job—babysitting, washing dishes at a neighborhood restaurant, pet sitting, anything that would allow her to start making a little money so she can start adding to her college savings account.

Cici is the youngest of three kids, and her parents have always made it clear that the kids will have to pay for a good chunk of their college tuition through loans, work study, and savings. Cici has seen her older siblings work one or two jobs during the school year, save like misers, and chip away at college expenses by taking college and Advanced Placement classes while they were in high school. So it's not news to her that she needs to get a job and start thinking about how she's going to pay for college. Still, she's already tired of her parents asking her what kind of job she wants. She's tired of them inviting her to take a look at a scholarship they found online. She's sick of thinking about the future, which is super far away, when she's more interested in thinking about her life right now.

Cici isn't the only teenager to resist her parents' talk about the years ahead. Even though she's only thirteen and high school graduation is a long way off, Cici is still well aware that there are big decisions coming at her soon. Her teachers and guidance counselors already remind students that the grades they get now give a hint at how they'll do in high school.

And it won't be long before Cici has to choose which of the three area high schools she wants to go to—a decision the adults in her life say will determine which college she gets in to and therefore what kind of job she'll get. It's all way too much to think about when you're thirteen and just hoping to make the volleyball team.

Cici's parents are in a tough spot, one that every parent of teenagers knows well. They are thinking about the future, trying to make sure they have the money in place to give their kids a helping hand on their way toward adulthood. At the same time, they are dealing with a child who is not even a little interested. Even conversations Cici's parents think are fairly safe—What kind of college do you want to go to? What kind of job do you see yourself having?—seem to blow up into shouting and slammed doors.

In spite of their insistence to the contrary, teenagers really are aware of the future. And they think about it more than we know. Of course, they probably aren't thinking much about the money part of the years ahead, but they are aware that many of the decisions they make now will have an impact on their lives down the road. What kind of impact? This is where teenagers need the adults in their lives to guide them gently into thinking about the future in more concrete ways. How you do that will depend a great deal on your teenager's Money Personalities.

Here's how to have conversations about the future if your teenager is a:

Saver

 Savers, especially teenage Savers, are all about the here and now. While they will be willing to talk about the future in general terms, their money concerns are focused on saving right now, not on building savings for college or a first apartment or travel after high school.

When you talk with your Saver about the years in front of her, you'll probably find that while she has dreams about what they might look like, she really doesn't have long-term plans for how she's going to get there. But ask her about her plans for next week, and she'll have them laid out in detail. That's because Savers are all about the immediate. They don't worry about what's coming, because they are too busy thinking about what's in front of them.

But when you get your Saver to look up and out at the long view, you'll be surprised at how adept she can be at making plans, especially when it comes to money. So ask your Saver questions now and then to get her engaged in dreaming about what might be next in her life. Don't over-whelm her by looking too far ahead or pushing her for concrete plans—those will come. Especially in her middle school and early high school years, keep the mood light and fun when you talk about the future. As it gets closer, you'll see her take steps to apply her saving skills to prepping for whatever comes next.

Spender

 Spenders live in the moment like nobody else. The future? Not interested. They want to squeeze every ounce of enjoyment out of this very second. But that doesn't mean they are oblivious. Naturally your Spender knows the future is com-ing, and he might even have ideas about how he wants it to play out. It's just that he doesn't have the mental space to really think about the details—there's way too much great stuff to think about and do right now.

When you talk about the years to come with your Spender, tread lightly. Keep these conversations as general as you can until his junior or senior year of high school, when it's time to start making real decisions. Until then, ask your teenager fun questions like "What do you think cars will be like by the time you're twenty-five?" or "What are three things you hope you get to do as part of your job one day?" Questions like these help you get an idea of what your teenager might be thinking about his future. They also get you both in the habit of having nonthreatening conversations that can pave the way for more concrete decisions in a few years.

On the money front, your Spender isn't going to save money, at least not enough to really make a difference in his future plans, so it will be crucial to talk to your Spender about necessary savings, especially college. Remember, your Spender lives in the moment and needs a little nudge to think more long-term. But you can still work with your teenager to help him get in the habit of making and sticking with a budget—one that leaves enough room for the occasional fun purchase. This is one of the most valuable skills you can teach a Spender to help him avoid a financial disaster when he heads out on his own.

Risk Taker

 Risk Takers have no trouble thinking about the future. It's being realistic that's the challenge. You probably can't get your Risk Taker teenager to stop talking about all the amazing stuff she's going to do once she's on her own. And that can work in your favor, especially when it comes to money decisions.

This is where the reality check comes in. As you and your teenager talk about her future plans, let her tell you all about her big ideas—studying abroad, a summer sailing in the Caribbean, starting up her own tutoring business. But instead of squelching those dreams, ask her to brainstorm ways she can start planning out the financial side of her vision. She might surprise you with how hard she's willing to work to turn her ideas into reality.

Security Seeker

If you want to talk about future plans with your Security Seeker, go right ahead. But be prepared to discover that he has everything worked out, from how he'll pay for school (down to which campus jobs he's going to apply for) to how much he'll need to make in his first job to be able to pay down his student loans in three years, to what kind of home he's hoping to purchase one day. Even if these are all speculation at this point, you can bet that when the time comes to put a real plan together, your Security Seeker will get it done.

Where your teenager needs your help, however, is in making room for the unknown and the unimagined. We adults know that life rarely follows a clear road map, so you'll need to help your Security Seeker get used to the idea that no matter how airtight his plans might be, he should expect some curves and potholes on his road to his safe, secure future.

You don't need to scare him with tales of friends whose kids didn't get into college or people you know who are still paying off their student loans twenty years after graduation. But do your best to remind your teenager that while it's great to have plans, the happiest people are those who leave a little room for those magical unplanned paths that take them to places they never dreamed they might go—a low-paying but deeply satisfying job, a semester abroad that doesn't help his major but could enrich his worldview, helping a friend start up a business even if that means paying off those loans over five years instead of three. Encourage him to make room in his plans for a little adventure.

Flyer

 Your Flyer might have all kinds of thoughts about the future, but the chances are good that these ideas are more about who will be part of her future, not what. She and her best friend want to go to the same college or get an apartment together after graduation. She wants to backpack through Spain with her Spanish pen pal. She wants to stay close to home so she can keep babysitting those darling kids down the street.

Whatever thoughts your Flyer has about the future, they are going to center on her relationships. You might even find that she's reluctant to talk about or think about the future, because it means her relationships will change. Of all the big changes ahead, that's the one that scares her the most.

As you make money decisions about the future with your Flyer, take her need to stay connected with old friends into consideration. If she's thinking about heading out of state for college, start setting aside money now for a few flights home, even if college is a few years away. Assure her that she will not only find ways to hang on to those friendships that really matter to her, but that she has all kinds of great relationships to look forward to.

Button Pushers for Parents

Saver

Unless your teenager is also a Saver, you're likely going to be irritated at her spending habits most of the time. But you might find that you get particularly frustrated when it comes to conversations about the future. You might see your teenager as irresponsible or flaky when it comes to money and have visions of her blowing through any money she does make down the road in less time than it takes her to make it.

Be careful not to assume that the money habits you see in your teenager now are the ones she'll carry into adulthood. Maturity and the realities of life can turn even the most careless Spender into a more thoughtful shopper. So avoid shaming your child because of her approach to money. Instead, pass on the great skills you have for finding good deals and planning ahead. These will serve her well no matter what her Money Personalities are.

Spender

Planning for your teenager's future is one thing. Having to hold back on your own spending right now is a whole different ball game.

Conversations about the future are full of money decisions that don't come easily to Spenders. So work with your parenting partner or even a financial planner to make sure you have plans in place to help your teenager take the next steps in life.

Making these plans happen is going to call for a lot of self-discipline for Spender parents. So try to think of the financial sacrifices you're making now as one more way you can give to your kids. Your generous nature will help you dig deep and do what's best for them.

Risk Taker

Risk Taker parents can get frustrated when they think their teenagers' future plans are too safe. College? Anyone can go to college. Why not spend a year in India or Latin America first? Why not get a VW van and take an epic road trip the summer between high school and college? Why not skip college and use that brain to start up a little business or two? These are the thoughts that run through a Risk Taker's mind, even if she never says them out loud.

So be mindful that your need for adventure might not be the same as your teenager's. Respect the vision he has for his own life and do your best to support that vision through careful financial planning and honest conversations with your teenager about his hopes and dreams.

Even if those dreams aren't as thrilling as you might hope, remember that the idea of leaving home and starting a new life on his own is a pretty great adventure for any teenager.

Security Seeker

 Your challenge here won't be the planning part. You have that covered. What's going to push your buttons is your teenager's reluctance to talk about those plans as often as you would like to.

Keep in mind that even a monthly chat about college plans can feel oppressive to a high school student who is already reminded every time she turns around that college is looming. Your ideas about what constitutes a meaningful conversation regarding the future and your teenager's aren't likely to be the same thing.

Still, you want to keep the lines of communication open between you and your teenager. So when you do want to discuss her future, start with light questions like, "Do you ever think about the kind of town you'd like to live in?" or "What do you think you'll be like when you're my age?" Try to avoid talking about money all the time. Instead, focus on your child's hopes and dreams for the future. Not only will this keep your relationship working well, it can actually help you plan more effectively. You'll get a sense of what kind of path your teenager might head down, meaning you won't end up with a medical school savings plan for the kid who wants to be an accountant.

Finally, watch out for your tendency to worry. Whether she tells you or not, your teenager has her own worries about the future. The last thing she needs is to have her parents remind her of all the things that could go wrong with her plans. So if you find yourself worrying that you haven't saved enough for college, take it up with your financial planner, not your teenager.

Flyer

 Flyer parents need to enlist the help of others when it comes to thinking about their kids' futures. Unless you have some solid money management skills to bring to the table, it's best for Flyers to work with a financial planner or even a school guidance counselor to sort through the money details of setting aside funds for your child's future. If you think you can do it yourself and that you'll get around to it one of these days, trust us, you will be the rare Flyer if you do.

It's not that Flyers can't figure these things out. Flyers aren't dumb; they just don't really think about money very often. The bigger issue is that Flyers are so invested in their relationships in the here and now that planning for the future isn't much of a priority. So let go of your pride and ask for help. Making the best plans you can for your kids is another way of nurturing the relationship you value so much.

17

Money Personality Goals for Ages 13–17

At this age, your child is starting to develop a more complex sense of identity. He's starting to see that he can be shy sometimes and outgoing at others, or silly with you and more serious with his friends. This process of getting to know themselves makes this a great time to help teenagers expand their Money Personalities to include some traits from the other Money Personalities. Savers can practice being more generous. Spenders can work on making more careful decisions. Building this balance into teenagers' Money Personalities will give them a leg up as they get closer to living on their own.

Goals for Savers

 Teenage Savers are great at saving their allowance or paychecks. They aren't so great at thinking about the future or being generous with their money. You can help your Saver develop some new money skills by setting up easy goals that move him outside of his own Money Personality.

You can teach your Saver teenager how to spend, take risks, and prioritize relationships over money by having him take a certain amount of money from his savings—let him choose how much—and asking him to think about someone he could spend that money on. He could take a buddy out to the movies, give it to the church or to a charity, buy a surprise gift for a sibling, maybe even take a risk with his money. Then talk about this process with him. Praise his efforts and encourage him to keep it up. Remind him that relationships and kindness are always going to be more valuable than money.

Goals for Spenders

 It's not easy for Spenders to save or invest their money. They live in a culture that wants them to spend it all, right now! You can make it easier for your Spender to learn how to save by setting low-key expectations for any allowance or income he has.

Set up a system in which 10 percent of his money goes into a savings account of some kind and 10 percent is given away to church or a charity. The remaining 80 percent is all his to do with it what he wants. Once he gets used to setting aside a portion of his income, he'll see that it's not too hard to have a great time on 80 percent.

Goals for Risk Takers

Remember, the operative word for your Risk Taker is *adventure.* If you try to rein it in too much, you'll only end up with a rebellious child. You can encourage responsibility and still give your teenager room for adventure. The secret is to tap into her creativity. Have your Risk Taker write down all the different kinds of work she could do to make money. She'll probably have a bunch of ideas—putting together a mowing business or starting an Internet business—but have her choose one that seems like it could work. Then help her see that she can make these things happen if she is careful with her spending, disciplined with her savings, and self-controlled enough to follow through with her idea. Get her moving on a business plan, and she'll start developing the skills she needs to save, plan for the future, and spend wisely.

Goals for Security Seekers

Getting your Security Seeker to live in the moment will be one of the best skills you can teach him. So encourage him to think about some short-term goals. What would he like to accomplish this semester outside of school? What's one school activity he has thought about trying but never has?

Encourage him to be spontaneous with his friends—call them out of the blue to play some basketball, head to a movie even though he has a math test in two weeks, try a new pizza place. As he moves out of his comfort zone a bit, he'll get more comfortable taking the occasional risk.

Goals for Flyers

 Your Flyer will need very concrete goals not only to develop some of the skills from those Money Personalities she doesn't have, but to develop those she *does* have as well. Take her to the bank and help her set up checking and savings accounts. Then, once a month, sit down with her to balance her checkbook and talk through her spending for the month to help her think about the next month's budget. What kinds of things does she tend to spend money on? What new expenses might she have in the coming month? Keep these conversations focused on short-term goals and expectations so she doesn't get overwhelmed with the money details.

Make It Happen!

SECTION 4

· · ·

Ages 18 and Beyond

18

Inside the Mind of Your Young Adult

Wouldn't it be great if you were done with the heavy lifting of parenthood once your kids turn eighteen? If you could just relax and enjoy their company and not worry about them anymore? Once you're done laughing—or crying—we want to look at some of the developmental issues happening in the lives of children as they become, well, not children anymore.

Katie is a perfect example. At twenty-one, she is in her final year of undergraduate work at a small college about two hours away from her hometown. She is a good student, has worked hard to get decent grades, and will graduate with a nursing degree. She will also graduate with a lot of debt.

It's not just student loans that are looming on the horizon. Katie got her first credit card when she was a freshman, and boy, has she used it! She has about $6,000 in debt on her card, enough that her parents have threatened to confiscate her card the next time she's home and hide it until she has paid off at least half of her bill.

On the plus side, Katie is earning a nursing degree and is highly likely to get a good job fairly soon after graduation. But even a good job isn't going to pay her enough to rent an apartment in the city, pay down her credit card debt and her loans, and have enough left for groceries, her phone bill, her car payment, and all the other expenses that come with a new life in a new place.

Katie isn't too worried about any of this. She has always been fairly independent and responsible, and she thinks she's going to be just fine once she graduates. Besides, she figures she can live with her parents for a few months while she gets settled into a new career, even if it means a forty-five-minute commute to the hospital where she is doing her training and hopes to get a job.

Katie's parents, of course, have slightly different expectations for Katie's post-college living situation. She's their youngest child, and they have spent her college years getting their house ready to sell so they can move into a smaller, maintenance-free town house. They've finally reached the life stage they've been planning for, and they are ready to retire, travel, and enjoy the end of college tuition payments.

Over Katie's fall break, her parents broached the subject of her future and their plans to move within the next year. It didn't go well. Katie didn't understand why she couldn't just live in the second bedroom of the new town house. But Katie's parents know why—their older son had lived at home for a year after college, and it was a bumpy experience, to say the least. They aren't interested in repeating the same fights with Katie.

Katie and her parents are stuck. Katie is well prepared for life on her own, but she's not in any hurry to be fully responsible for herself. Her parents are torn between wanting to help their youngest child get her feet under her and feeling like the more help they give, the longer it will take for her to really grow up. Do they push her out of the nest and make her fly or nurture her a little longer?

Katie's Money Personalities are also playing a role in this tension. Katie is a Spender/Security Seeker. Her parents know she's responsible. She has a plan for earning money and paying off her debts and loans, and her parents know she'll stick to that plan. But they also know she likes to shop and that having her own apartment is likely to bring with it even more spending and debt.

Once kids reach the age of eighteen, they legally enter into adulthood. But every parent of a young adult knows that these kids are far from living or thinking like mature, responsible adults. In fact, studies show that more and more young adults are either still living with their parents or moving home after college. A 2011 Pew Foundation study found that 53 percent of young people between the ages of eighteen and twenty-four live with their parents. Among adults ages twenty-five to twenty-nine, that number drops a bit to 41 percent. Still, it means the odds are awfully good that if you have a child in this age group, your empty nest might not be empty for long.

There are many reasons why young adults return home—the huge burden of student loans and the challenges of finding a job right out of college chief among them. We'll offer ideas for working through these and other situations in the coming chapters. But even apart from the financial details of the return flight to the nest, there are several developmental issues at play for this age group. Being aware of those issues can help parents work through the money conversations that are an essential piece of helping your young adult children get settled in the "real world."

As parents, we have to constantly remind ourselves that the "real world" our children are jumping into is very different from the one we found ourselves in. Not only is this generation facing a difficult economy but they are much more transient than we were, are far less likely to get married and start a family in their twenties, and will most certainly change careers more frequently than we did. So they don't think about their futures as something solid and settled. They don't have one future; they have a bunch.

While that can feel exciting, it's also overwhelming for a lot of young adults. Unlike us, they aren't coming out of college with degrees that translate to particular jobs. Some experts say that a student entering college right now will end up with a job that hasn't been invented yet. Our kids won't necessarily have to live near where they work. They won't have to work eight to five or only on weekdays. They will have options for their work/family balance that we never dreamed of. That means that our kids have to make decisions that weren't on the table for us.

And in spite of the evidence that young people are returning home in droves, it's a mistake to assume they are unmotivated and irresponsible. Read any article about world-changing businesses or cultural movers and shakers and you'll discover that a lot of the people making the biggest impact on the world right now are under thirty. Young adults might not have the maturity that our grandparents did at their age, but they are still full of big ideas and all kinds of passion and energy for making the world a better place.

When you talk with your young adult, you might find that he's hesitant to get a "normal" job because he has a vision for something different, something bigger than just working to earn a paycheck. This idealism might seem silly to some of us, but it's the dreaminess and willingness to step into the unknown that makes young adults the kind of people who really do shake things up for the better. This is the time for your child to move somewhere unexpected, or travel for a year, or try his hand at selling his art or joining a band or starting a business or whatever it is that inspires him right now. As hard as it might be for you to step back and let your young adult try something unusual, that's exactly what you need to do.

Katie and her parents have everything they need to work through the challenges that are hitting them right now. They have a good relationship, they are aware of each other's expectations, and they have fairly concrete plans for the immediate future. That means they know each other's Money Personalities and have a good idea of where they tend to clash when they talk about money decisions. They are well equipped to find a way to help Katie take her first steps into adulthood. It won't be easy, and they won't find a solution in a day or even a month. But keeping the lines of communication open and working together is key to them still liking each other, no matter what kind of living arrangements they end up with.

In the coming chapters, we'll dig into ideas for guiding your young adult through some of the big money decisions that come with this stage of life. As we do, keep these developmental themes in mind along with the financial goals for each Money Personality.

Relationships Are Everything

No matter which Money Personalities your child has, her need for healthy, meaningful relationships—with friends and family—will be the driving force in her life right now. Young adults live in a fairly constant state of transition. They typically leave high school and home and start some sort of post–high school education or career. They move out of the house (at least for a little while). They start over in a new city, at a new job, with new friends. Even if they stick around, their friends leave, and they have no choice but to start over with a new routine.

You'll see your child's Money Personalities in her efforts to establish deeper friendships and work through the shifts in her relationship with you. For example, a Spender will take advantage of her increased freedom to go out to dinner with friends, shop with a buddy, travel, or decorate her dorm room—all expressions of her Spender Money Personality.

The shifts in her relationships also mean that this is a crucial stage in your relationship with your young adult child. For the most part, your connection will be the most stable, trustworthy part of his life for a while, especially if he's leaving home or starting a new job or moving back home. You are the solid foundation that helps him manage the seemingly constant changes in his life. So keep this in mind as you work through any money decisions together. Your child might want to act like he doesn't need you anymore, but emotionally, yours is the most important relationship he has right now.

He's More Responsible than You Think

This is so hard for parents to accept, especially when we see our young adult children make decisions we would never make. We look at the way they spend money or the way they choose a major or the people they date and wonder what on earth they are thinking. But this is the stage when, unless they are about to do something immoral or illegal, we have to let our young adult children make their own decisions.

Yes, we can weigh in. Yes, we can try to change their minds. Yes, we can tell them what we think. And if your child wants to drop out of college after you've been paying his tuition for three years, you had better believe you should be upset. But the bottom line is that you can't force a twenty-year-old to do what you want him to do. So tell him he needs to pay you back or tell him he'll have to fund his own Plan B. Tell him whatever you need to, and then breathe deeply because he's still going to forge his own path, just like you did, just like we did, just like everyone has to do sooner or later.

Yet even young adults who make dumb decisions will surprise you at their willingness to take responsibility for themselves. Most people like growing up. They like being independent and will do what it takes to remain independent once they've gotten a taste of sweet freedom. So your child might make a bad decision. He might spend too much on his first car or accept too little for his first job. But look for the good in his decisions and acknowledge his efforts to act responsibly when you see them. Think about his Money Personalities and use that information to help you understand him a bit better.

Failure Is an Option

All parents worry about their young adult children failing out in the real world. And every young adult worries about it too. We all know there are no guarantees about the future, and your young adult is keenly aware of this also. So you probably don't need to remind your child about the risks of whatever she's doing. She knows. She has heard the statistics and watched her friends stumble and fall ahead of her. Young adults know more about what they're facing than we think they do, and while they often seem naive as they forge ahead, it could be that their optimism is the only coping strategy they have to keep themselves applying for jobs or looking at schools or moving on with new friends.

Your child might stumble a little too. It will be hard to watch, but it's a necessary part of learning how to make one's own way in the world. Your Flyer child might get taken advantage of. Your Spender child might end up with serious debt. Your Saver might miss out on the adventures that come with being a young adult. You can't stop these things from happening, but you can—and should—help your child process her struggles and mistakes.

Talk with her about what went wrong. Help her think about ways to change the outcome next time. Rescue her if you need to, but be careful about stepping in with your checkbook or your great advice at every challenge. Instead, encourage her to develop the skills she needs to keep it from happening again. If you keep your child tethered to you—emotionally or financially—it will be that much harder for her to leave the nest and build a life of her own.

19

Financial Independence

Jay is a sophomore in college, and he's loving it. He's getting decent grades, making good friends, and having an awesome time. His first year was a little bumpy; it took a semester and maybe a little more for him to figure out that he had to actually go to class if he was going to keep his grades up. And since he knows he's probably going to head to graduate school for an MBA a year or two after college, he's working hard to do well in class. Everything is humming along, and he has found his niche at school.

For the most part, Jay's parents have been thrilled with how well he has adjusted to college life. Jay was a little shy during his teen years, and they worried he would have a hard time making friends. But being away from home has helped Jay blossom into a more confident, friendly, and funny young man who has had no problem meeting people.

The only problem has been money. It turns out that

despite being a smart guy, Jay has no concept of how to handle money. During his freshman year, his parents put a few hundred bucks in Jay's checking account every other month. Since his meals and housing were paid for already, they figured he really only needed spending money for the occasional outing with friends. They didn't expect Jay to blow through $100 in a weekend—fast food, movies, concerts, football games, clothes. It seemed like Jay couldn't stop spending. How he had the time for all this spending was a mystery to his parents.

The summer between his freshman and sophomore years, Jay and his parents had a little "come to Jesus" talk about Jay's spending habits. His parents decided that if Jay couldn't curb his spending, then he would have to start spending his own money. He got a summer job as a filing clerk for a small business in town—good experience that paid pretty well—and turned all of his paychecks over to his parents. They put him on a tight budget and made sure he was saving money for the school year.

All of this seemed like a great idea until November of Jay's sophomore year. That's when Jay's parents get a phone call that goes something like this:

"Um, Dad? Do you think you guys could put some money in my checking account?"

"What happened to your savings from the summer? That was supposed to get you through most of the year."

"Yeah, I know. But it turns out I've needed to spend more this year than I expected."

"Spend more on what, Jay?"

And that's when the excuses start—books cost more than

he thought, the guys wanted to take a road trip to see a football game and he had to help pay for gas and a hotel room, he needed some stuff for his dorm room, he was sick of campus food and had been getting pizza a few times a week.

Clearly, Jay is a Spender/Flyer. Not only does he love to spend money, but he really doesn't think about money very often. He's much more interested in the relationships he's building and will happily spend money he doesn't have to maintain them. Despite having some healthy savings built up to start the semester, Jay has left himself broke and back in the same empty money boat he was in last year.

Jay's parents aren't sure what to do. If they bail him out, he might never learn to limit his spending. But they realize he can't really handle his own finances. Do they let him sink and figure it out? When is it time to let go and when is it time to step in?

When your child graduates from high school and ventures into whatever comes next—college, trade school, a job, travel, volunteer work—he will get his first real taste of financial independence. What that means exactly will vary from family to family, but we find that most parents gradually hand over control of the finances by the time their child hits his early twenties.

These years are fraught with growing pains—for all of you. Like Jay's parents, many parents of young adults are torn between helping too much and not helping enough. For young people like Jay, the challenges of starting over, making new friends, figuring out how to balance school and work and a social life, and working through huge decisions about their majors and careers and relationships are more than they can handle. Dealing with money is just one more thing that feels overwhelming.

But growing pains and all, this is the time to help your young adult truly learn to take care of his own finances and make his own money decisions, even when they seem ridiculous to you. You don't need to cut your kid off when he turns eighteen, but you can and should use these years to slowly hand off the last of your involvement in your child's money decisions.

As you do, keep your young adult's Money Personalities in mind. Now that your child is older and making more of his own money choices, you'll have far more opportunities to see these Money Personalities in action. Use what you see to help tailor your approach to letting go of your child's needs.

Here's how to encourage financial independence if your young adult is a:

Saver

 Scott's college roommate was a Saver, and while he had no trouble budgeting his finances down to the penny, he did deal with a lot of worry and anxiety about money. Your Saver will likely deal with that same kind of worry, especially as he gets used to being responsible for his own money.

The odds are good that your Saver has been developing great money habits for a long time now and that you're not concerned that he's going to blow through a semester's worth of spending money in his first month at school. But he might not be as confident as you are. Whatever this stage of life involves for your Saver, it's filled with money decisions he has never had to make before, such as how much rent is too much rent and just how often can he order Chinese food before it breaks his weekly budget.

The best way to ease your Saver's concerns is to encourage him to do what Savers do best—research the options, look for good deals, and skimp on what doesn't matter so that he has enough money for what does. Let your Saver know that you are confident he will take good care of his finances and that if an unexpected expense comes up or he miscalculates, you'll be there to help him work through it. Even if you're not in a position to help your child out financially, your emotional support and practical advice will mean the world to him.

Spender

 It's no secret that we live in a materialistic society. If you want to spend money, there are endless opportunities to do so. And this is particularly true for young people venturing out on their own for the first time. Not only will your Spender now have more free time and independence than ever before, she will have absolutely no one to ask her how much she's spending on school sweatshirts and dorm room décor and late-night pizzas. You might get a general idea once a month if you're still holding the purse strings, but those daily decisions will come and go without anyone holding your Spender accountable. And that's a disaster waiting to happen.

Life after high school is a Spender's paradise. Your young adult will need lots of guidance and preparation before you send her off to college or her first job to help her understand the very real dangers that can come from overspending. Help her realize that she can still spend money on fun stuff but that she needs to pick and choose so she's not throwing money at everything that catches her attention.

You also need to warn your Spender about credit cards. Credit card companies looooove young adults. These companies know that young people are excited to be on their own, eager to spend money, and short on cash. So they will hand out credit cards to any kid who can sign up, counting on kids to spend far more than they can afford. We know of so many young adults who are deep in credit card debt before they even get their first real job, and they often find it almost impossible to recover.

Risk Taker

 Now that your Risk Taker has moved out of your house, you're probably simultaneously breathing a sigh of relief and lying awake at night wondering what dangerous things your child might be up to at that very moment. Life with a Risk Taker is always an adventure, but now that your child is venturing into adulthood, you really can relax a bit. Yes, he'll probably still do a few things that wake you up with worry, but Risk Takers have a way of moving beyond literal risks and finding their thrills in slightly more mature ways.

Your college-age Risk Taker will probably change

majors—a lot! Or maybe yours has decided to travel through Europe for a year or spend some time in the Peace Corps after college graduation. Certainly all of these have varying levels of risk, but they are part of what makes life interesting and fulfilling for your Risk Taker.

Of course there will always be a money component to your Risk Taker's decisions. Changing majors late in the game can often mean adding on a semester or two of college. Traveling obviously takes money, and working with an organization like the Peace Corps means forgoing a bigger income in the name of helping others. That doesn't mean you should deny your Risk Taker the chance to do these things. It just means you'll need to be intentional about talking through the money component with him or at least make sure he's considering the financial piece of these decisions along with the thrill factor.

Security Seeker

Your Security Seeker won't have any trouble getting through college in four years. She might even get out in two, because she has been taking AP classes and college-level courses in high school as part of her perfect plan for the perfect future. So your Security Seeker probably doesn't need much help from you when it comes to making money decisions during these first few years of independence. She'll know just what she needs to do in order to make all her plans fall into place.

What she will need, however, is a nudge toward letting go of her control over that plan and making room for some unexpected fun. If she's too focused on graduating in three and a half years, or applying for the perfect internship, she might miss the chance to study abroad for a semester or spend her summer working at a youth camp.

Encourage your Security Seeker to hold her plans a bit more loosely than she might be comfortable with. Part of being a good planner is knowing that life hands you unexpected twists and turns and being confident that you can handle them. Help your young adult find opportunities to test her resilience and spontaneity. Those are skills she'll need as she keeps walking into adulthood.

Flyer

 Your Flyer is going to love his new independence. While he might be nervous about starting this next stage of life, he's also going to be excited about the potential for new friendships and new experiences. What he won't think about at all is money.

Flyers tend to be dreamers when it comes to the future. As they move from thinking about life after high school or college to really living it, they have a hard time moving from their dreams to reality. So your Flyer might have his heart set on moving to a big city, getting a supercool apartment with a few friends, and finding an awesome job. And he really thinks it's going to play out just like that. So he needs your help—not to crush those dreams but to show him how to make them a bit more realistic.

You can do that by tuning in to his secondary Money Personality. He might not show much interest in money decisions, but if you can work with the strengths of his other Money Personality, you're going to see him make good decisions when they come along. So if he's a Flyer/Saver, tap into his ability to find a good deal. Help him research the average rental rate of an apartment in the city he's looking at. Which neighborhoods are more affordable? Which ones will be out of reach? If he's a Flyer/Spender, help him think through ways he can make enough money to pay for his living expenses and still have enough for fun stuff. Look over our suggestions for the other Money Personalities for more ideas on how to help your Flyer take steps toward financial independence.

Button Pushers for Parents

Saver

 The cost of college, of housing, heck, even the cost of gas is enough to drive a Saver to despair. As you watch your adult child make what are likely to be some questionable decisions about money, you'll want to jump in with advice and maybe even some scolding words. But don't.

This is a delicate stage in the parent/child relationship. Remember that your young adult is acutely aware of how easily she might fail on her path to success. So she's looking to you for signs that you believe she has what it takes to make a life for herself. If you're constantly reminding her how hard you worked to save for her tuition, or how expensive everything is, or how you think she's making bad money decisions, she's going to stop talking to you about those decisions altogether. And that's when she'll be in real trouble. Your young adult needs your expertise and good ideas about saving money, but she also needs you to let her make a few dumb mistakes and encourage her as she works to correct them.

Spender

Spenders have no trouble spending money on their kids. Instead, your hot button is making sure you know when to stop. It's essential that you let your adult child make his own money choices and live with the results of those choices. We know lots of Spenders who keep bailing their kids out of financial trouble. While their intentions might be good, they risk hamstringing their kids just when they need to start standing on their own two feet.

There are times when giving your young adult financial help is the right move. If you can help him avoid crippling debt by paying down his credit card bill, pay it for him, and have him pay you back over the course of several months. He needs first and last months' rent to secure a decent apartment in a safe part of town? Help if you can. But if you rescue your young adult every time he empties his bank account or commits to paying for something he can't afford, he'll never get the chance to work through those problems on his own and learn how to make better decisions.

Risk Taker

No matter what your young adult is up to in these first years on her own—college, work, travel—it will be hard for you to be a bystander. You'll either find yourself antsy because your child is in a structured environment like college for such a long time and you're eager to help her do more, or you'll find yourself jealous of the adventures that await your child as she ventures into the unknown.

Either way, make sure you're not imposing your Money Personality on your young adult. She needs to make her own way in life, and she is going to make different choices than those you might want her to make. If she has settled on a major, don't keep throwing other options at her. If she has started on a career path, don't e-mail her asking if she wants to spend three months in a kibbutz with you. If she's starting to make some good money, don't pressure her to invest in some business venture you just heard about. Remember, she's looking for your nod of approval to let her know she's capable of making her own good choices.

Security Seeker

You worked hard to get your child to this point, and you might find yourself wondering what's next. Since helping to launch your kids into adulthood is typically one of your biggest financial goals as a Security Seeker, you can find yourself at a bit of a loss when that time actually comes. Be mindful that your empty nest syndrome might include a bit of financial uncertainty. Give yourself some time to set new goals and you'll feel a bit more settled.

In terms of your young adult children, make sure you give them some time too. Security Seekers like a plan. Most young adults don't. There's no point in pressuring your college freshman to choose a major—that time will come.

You'll need to reorient yourself a bit and remember that these young adult years are the time when your child is figuring out what kind of plan he might like for his life, not the time when he has it all figured out. Be patient, do more listening than talking, and when the time comes to help your young adult think about his more immediate future, he'll still trust you enough to turn to you for help.

Flyer

 Launching a child out of the house and into adulthood is hard on Flyer parents. The changes in the parent/child relationship that come with this life stage take a lot of getting used to for every parent, but Flyers in particular can find themselves feeling lonely and adrift.

On the money front, this can turn into a kind of financial codependence. In an effort to stay connected with your adult child, you might find yourself throwing money at the problem—taking her out to eat whenever she's in town, offering to fly her home just because you miss her, buying her a car so she can come and visit more easily. If you can afford these ways of staying close and your child is on board, great. But be careful you don't let your need to keep that relationship exactly the same as it has been become a hurdle for your child to leap over as she moves into adulthood.

20

Firsts

Eric is one semester away from getting his associate's degree from a community college. It has taken him almost three years, because he has paid his own way through school by stringing together a handful of jobs and living at home. It has been a pretty good arrangement but has also been exhausting. Work and school, work and school—that has been Eric's life for the last three years.

Living at home has made economic sense, and his parents have been pretty good about letting Eric come and go as he likes. But still, he's a twenty-one-year-old guy living at home when he would like to be a twenty-one-year-old guy living anywhere other than with his family in his hometown. Two of his best friends from high school are getting ready for their senior year of college. The three of them have talked about getting a place together near the college. They would finish school, find jobs, and have a great setup for the next few years.

Eric is psyched about the idea, but he's also pretty nervous. He hates to admit it, but he's kind of worried about living on his own. He has always been good with money—he doesn't like to waste money on stuff he doesn't need. But he knows his share of a three-bedroom apartment will be at least $400 rent. And he really has no idea how to find a decent place. He has heard horror stories about people putting down money on an apartment only to find out there's no unit available. Or getting roped into a two-year lease on a dump with roaches and mice.

And this whole plan depends on Eric getting a job. He has been working for years, but not in the kind of jobs that can help you earn a real living. He can still get health care through his parents, but it would be nice to have some benefits like paid vacation days and normal hours. He has some ideas about the kind of work he would like to do, but beginning the process of finding job openings, putting together a résumé, and interviewing can be overwhelming.

As ready as he is to move on, there's a part of Eric that would be okay with staying at his parents' house, working his two jobs, and just saving money a little longer. He could actually have a social life, could maybe volunteer with his old youth group, and would use the time to find a good job. His buddies could find another roommate for the year, and he would move in with them after they graduate.

But Eric's parents aren't too keen on that idea. It has been nice having Eric around. He has helped them with things around the house and been easy to live with. But they know he has to get out there and start making a life for himself. They don't want to push him out of the nest, but they worry that if they don't give him a little kick, he might stay there indefinitely.

Eric is at a big turning point, one every young adult faces sooner or later. He's about to look for his first real job, find his first apartment, experience his first time living on his own. No matter how mature or independent a young adult is, these "firsts" can be daunting.

The biggest challenge for young adults stepping into their first this or that is the fear factor. Remember that young adults wrestle with the fear of failing. They know there's a lot riding on these firsts, and they worry they will somehow blow it—accept a job that doesn't pay enough, end up in a cruddy apartment, get stuck with a roommate who doesn't pay his share of the rent, date the wrong person, or buy a lemon of a car. Adults know these are the kinds of learning experiences everyone goes through sooner or later, that they are just part of life; but for young adults, these setbacks feel like personal failures, like signs that they aren't cut out for adulthood.

That fear can be paralyzing. It's enough to keep a smart, capable guy like Eric stuck in his parents' house for another year or more even though he has everything he needs to move on. And it's hard for parents to know how hard to push. Some young adults really do need a little more time to mature to the point where they can make good decisions, particularly good money decisions. If parents push too hard, do they doom their kids to failure? Or does it take a little dose of failure to motivate kids to make better decisions in the future?

Eric, who is a Saver and Security Seeker, is the kind of guy who will usually make good, stable, smart money decisions. He's not likely to blow his first paycheck on new basketball shoes or buy a clunker car on a whim. But his Money Personalities bring about different fears. The Saver in him is worried that his new life will be too expensive, that he won't be able to make enough money to survive on his own. The Security Seeker in him worries that his plans might not come through—he would like them to be set in stone before he moves forward.

Every young adult has her own fears about these firsts, so as you talk with your child about getting that first job or first apartment or first car, do your best to address her specific fears and help her develop a plan for how she'll deal with the failures and challenges that will inevitably come along. Remind her that no one goes through life on a smooth path and that success isn't about never failing—it's about how you recover from those failures and move on. We like to say that "God doesn't steer a parked car"—life happens when we set a course and get moving.

Here's how to talk about "firsts" if your young adult is a:

Saver

 Young adult Savers like Eric are a funny paradox. They are the most likely to avoid financial disaster in these years of starting out, and yet they are usually the most concerned about it. Savers will put off some of the necessary expenses of adult life—finding a place to live, getting a car, buying professional clothes—because they hate to spend more than they think is necessary. They will look for deals, try to negotiate, and just walk away from an apartment or a car if they think the deal's not good enough.

While some of the need to get a deal is just part of being

a Saver, you need to keep an eye out so it does not become an excuse to put off difficult decisions. Your Saver is going to have to spend money sooner or later, whether he likes it or not. And he'll have to accept that sometimes it's better to spend more up front to save money later. A cheap car is going to be expensive to keep running. A cheap apartment is going to be a money pit if he has to add space heaters or window AC units or can't make meals in the kitchen because the oven is a fire hazard.

Help your Saver tap into his innate ability to save money on things that don't matter as much to him—maybe cool shoes or tech gadgets or eating out—so he can afford to pay for the things he truly needs—a decent place to live, a reliable car, nice clothes for work. If you have a budget plan, show him how you've divvied up your income to pay for living expenses and encourage him to work out his own budget so he can settle in with the idea that he can support himself and still live well within his means.

Spender

 A Spender is going to get super excited about all of these firsts, particularly those that involve buying new stuff. A first apartment translates into buying furniture, bedding, pots and pans, and rugs and lamps. And that's nothing but awesome for a Spender. A first job is an invitation to buy new clothes, eat lunch at a restaurant every day, grab coffee on the way to work. Every new opportunity brings new ways of spending money.

So you'll need to help your Spender set some realistic expectations. A first apartment isn't meant to look like a magazine spread. We know a Spender couple who thought they needed to buy all new furniture for their first apartment. It took them ten years to pay off those bills. Thankfully, most Spenders will find that decorating on a budget can be just as fun as buying all new stuff. Encourage your Spender to set some limits for how much she'll spend on work clothes, transportation, and household goods. She will probably blow right through them now and then, but that's part of learning how to balance the wants and needs of adult life.

And be aware that just because your Spender is excited about these firsts doesn't mean she's not a little afraid of them too. Spenders know they have a tendency to overdo it when it comes to money, and if your young adult is venturing into her first real job and therefore her first real experience with a decent amount of disposable income, she might very well be worried that she'll get herself into money trouble. So get her to talk about any fears she might have about managing her money and living on her own. Make it clear you are always available to talk through both her challenges and her successes.

Risk Taker

 In general, Risk Takers appear to be pretty fearless people. But it's not that they don't feel any fear; it's that they thrive on fear. So you might see your Risk Taker jumping into adulthood with both feet—moving to a city he has never been to, nabbing a place to live from Craigslist sight unseen, not worrying too much about getting a job until he has picked a place to live. Some of this might work out; some of it won't. And that's fine with the Risk Taker.

But he'll still have concerns about ending up stuck in a lousy housing situation or not liking his job. He'll still worry that he won't have enough money to fund his big ideas. He'll still be a little afraid that his life will be dull and boring.

You can help your Risk Taker prepare for the firsts that are coming by having him find some balance between planning and letting some decisions be spontaneous. Housing? It's best not to be surprised by a housing situation—a bad landlord, disrespectful or disruptive roommates, or a dangerous neighborhood can all add a tremendous amount of stress to your young adult's life, stress that makes it hard to move forward with other decisions. But not having the perfect job lined up? That's something he can manage—Risk Takers don't mind working just to get a paycheck, because they can always find adventure somewhere else.

Help your Risk Taker get a few of his plans in place before he sets out, and then find a way to make yourself comfortable with the uncertain parts of his immediate future. Letting him take some chances without your input might be one of the "firsts" you're afraid of, but just like your young adult, you'll make it through just fine.

Security Seeker

 These are the young adults most prone to something we call "paralysis by analysis." In their need to have every part of the future mapped out before they take a step forward, Security

Seekers can get stuck and never move at all. Like Eric in the example at the beginning of the chapter, Security Seekers can get obsessed with the "what-ifs" that come along with all the firsts they are experiencing. *What if I don't get a job? What if my housing falls through? What if my car breaks down?* And when they get obsessed, they stall out.

Your Security Seeker will need a reality check from you. But try not to be unrealistic in your efforts to quell her fears about the future—Security Seekers know things go wrong all the time, and if you try to convince them everything will be rosy, they won't believe you. So talk honestly about what could happen and how he can deal with it. If he doesn't get the job he wants, what's his backup plan? If his housing situation isn't ideal, what can he do to make it better?

And let him know it's normal to worry a little. Tell him about a time when your plans didn't work out and you had to recalibrate. Most of all, help him put his fears into perspective. If he lives his life based on fear and worry, he will miss all the goodness waiting for him. Help him learn to trust both the plans he has made and his ability to recover when those plans don't pan out.

Flyer

 The Flyer will leap into these firsts with big ideas about how awesome it's all going to be. What she won't have is any kind of plan or perspective on what it takes to settle into adult life. Since your Flyer will be focused on the relationships in her life—even more so than the average young adult—she is as likely to base her future plans on whom she wants to live with as she is on what she wants to do.

That's not the worst thing in the world. If she has good friends to live with, that's one less "first" you need to worry about. But if she's rejecting solid job leads or other options because they might disrupt her relationships, talk to her about her decisions and help her weigh the pros and cons, including the money issues involved.

This is also a good time to encourage your Flyer to find a mentor or other adult who can offer her good advice about jobs, relationships, and so forth. Flyers do best when they have people in their lives they can trust to help them process decisions. Those people don't always have to be their parents. Another adult or two who know and love your child can be a great support system for her as she makes her way into adult life.

Button Pushers for Parents

This parade of "firsts" is going to be rough on you, mostly because every first involves some sort of money decision. Everything will feel like it costs more than it should. And you'll find yourself pushing your young adult to go cheaper on everything, from rent to phone packages to groceries. But trust us when we say you have to resist that urge.

Saver

 Saver parents are a huge asset to young adults making these significant money decisions. You'll know when a car is too expensive or an apartment is going to be out of reach on a starting salary. So when you see genuine opportunities to reduce your child's expenses, feel free to say something. But you can't nickel-and-dime your young adult to death. She might want to pay for cable even though you never would. She might want to get a fancy coffee drink at the drive-through every morning, something so far off your radar you didn't know there were drive-through coffee shops. Let her make these choices for herself. Trust her to find ways to reduce her costs if she finds that she's spending too much. This is the time to start letting your child make her own money decisions, even when they are different from yours.

Spender

 Every young adult wishes they had a Spender parent. You're going to have a great time outfitting your child's first apartment, helping him pick out an interview suit, and looking at used cars. It's like a free pass to spend and give all at the same time. And while we would never tell a Spender not to help out his child in a pinch, we do caution Spender parents to step gently into their children's lives at this stage.

These firsts are an opportunity for your young adult to find out how to make his way in the world. If you jump in with a handout every time he is struggling or needs something, he's never going to figure out how to balance his own wants and needs with his income. Since Spenders are eager givers, consider this chance to succeed and fail on his own a gift you're giving your child. It might not be his favorite gift, especially if he has come to expect the parental bailout, but it will be the ultimate gift that keeps on giving.

Risk Taker

This stage of a young adult's life is a lot of fun for Risk Taker parents, because it's a chance to be part of your child's big adventures. You can get a vicarious rush out of the possibilities in front of your child, so much so that you need to make sure you're not pushing him in a direction he doesn't want to go just because it sounds awesome to you.

Risk Takers also need to watch out for the tendency to keep their kids from "settling." Not every young adult is looking for a first job that lets him travel the globe. He might be perfectly happy to take that offer for a solid administrative job at a marketing firm in the suburbs. So make sure you are encouraging your young adult to make the decisions that work for him, even if they seem a little boring to you.

Security Seeker

This is a rough stage of life for Security Seeker parents. It's hard enough for Security Seekers to deal with the uncertainties that might be part of their own lives. It's even harder when you're dealing with the unknown future of your precious child. The temptation for you will be to plan everything for your child, even though that's the worst thing you can do.

As tough as it might be, Security Seekers need to channel their worry into productive advice. Your young adult probably has some ideas about what she needs to make her way, but you will be the ultimate resource for helping her make some concrete decisions about these firsts. Sit down together to research job openings, rental properties, used cars, whatever it is she needs. And help her think long-term. Once she gets that job, talk with her about insurance and retirement—if she starts good saving habits now, she's going to be in great shape for retirement. Use what you know to launch your child into her firsts with the tools she needs to build on these early years.

Flyer

 If you're a Flyer, these years can be a lot of fun. Your young adult is building new relationships, figuring out more about himself, and building a life for himself. It's the kind of stuff parents wait for. But you'll also find yourself struggling with the transition in your role as a parent. The bottom line is that your child is finally leaving for good and isn't going to need you the way he used to.

It can be tempting for Flyer parents to try to hold on to their adult children by tugging at some financial strings. You'll offer to take your child shopping for his apartment because it means you get to spend time together. Or you'll treat him to lunch every Friday or let him use your car or let him live at home indefinitely just to keep those ties strong. All of that is fine if you can afford it and your adult child is still making most of these decisions independently. But if you see that your need to keep him close is preventing him from really stepping into his own life, it's time to back up. Yes, your relationship will be different from now on, but it might also be stronger and richer than ever.

Debt

Kevin is a freshman at a big state university. He is walking through the student union one early spring afternoon and sees a cute girl sitting at a table. She has pretty eyes and a huge smile that she aims right at Kevin. And not only is she cute, but she has a stack of two-pound bags of M&M's sitting on the table next to her.

Needless to say, Kevin is intrigued. He wanders over to the table to find out this lovely girl's name and what he has to do for a bag of those M&M's. Turns out, Shana wants him to sign up for a credit card. Once he fills out the application, the M&M's are his (her phone number, not so much). He fills it out, signs on the dotted line, takes his candy, and heads to class.

A week later, Kevin has his first credit card. And boy does he have a good time with it. By the end of the semester, he has racked up $1,200 in debt. And he thinks it's awesome that he only has to pay $35 a month for it!

Then summer comes. The bill is forwarded to Kevin's

house, where his dad gets the mail. The afternoon Kevin's credit card bill arrives, Kevin's dad sits him down and explains how credit cards work and what Kevin has done by getting one—the word *deep* comes up. Kevin slowly begins to realize that not only does he not have the $1,200, but now he actually owes more than that, thanks to that nice little 17 percent interest added to his bill.

Kevin's dad says, "Well, you got yourself into this. You'll need to get yourself out of it." It is clear to Kevin that one summer job isn't going to be enough, and he spends the rest of his break working long hours at two jobs to pay off his debt and put some money away for the coming semester. It isn't a great summer.

Kevin is a Spender. And credit card companies love Spenders, especially young adult Spenders who really have no idea what it means to have a credit card. While it doesn't feel like it at the time, Kevin is fortunate that his dad pushes him to pay that card off right away. It's all too common for young adults to dig themselves deeper and deeper into debt before they even have stable jobs to pay off that debt. It will come back to haunt them when they need a good credit rating to rent an apartment or get a car loan.

Credit cards aren't the only debt that saddle young adults. Fidelity Investments' second Cost-Conscious College Graduates Study found that 2013 college graduates were facing an average debt of more than $35,000 when they left school—a combination of student loans, credit card debt, and money owed to family members. That's a mind-boggling number for anyone, much less a young person just starting out in life. At that rate, goals like owning a house, starting a business, even getting married become increasingly out of reach.

Obviously it is important that parents talk about debt early in this stage of a child's life. Talking about debt after it has been accumulated is still important, but then it's a triage conversation meant to stop the bleeding. If your child is still in her late teens or early twenties, it's not too late to put some preventative measures into place that can help your child come in under that average level of debt.

Here's how to talk about debt if your young adult is a:

Saver

A Saver isn't likely to run up big credit card debt—even if he has a credit card, he probably pays it off every month—but even the most avid Savers can't completely avoid debt if they've taken out student loans. The good news is that Savers are very well equipped to whittle down that debt once they have an income. They will make it priority number one to get that debt paid off and out of their lives.

As you look at ways to keep a lid on debt with your Saver, have him think about ways he can keep his loans under control. Maybe he can add a work-study job to his academic mix or find cheaper options for some of his classes—community colleges and online schools often have classes that can fulfill core requirements at other colleges at a fraction of the cost. If that's not an option, help him accept that some debt is not a big deal. Debt is a dirty word for Savers, but when he recognizes that it's not always avoidable, he'll get over the frustration of having it and figure out how to pay it off.

Spender

Setting expectations about money is crucial for your Spender. Whether it's a credit card or how she's spending her loan money, you'll need to stay involved with her spending before she gets herself into trouble.

If your Spender wants a credit card, we suggest it be a joint account with you and/or your parenting partner. Have your child pay you, not the credit card company, so you can keep track of what she's spending and help her develop the discipline she needs to pay off that bill each month. For other Money Personalities, a credit card can be a great way to build a credit history. But for Spenders, especially those just getting used to being on their own, it can be a nightmare.

If your Spender already has a huge chunk of debt, help her put together a plan for paying it down as quickly as she can. Even though young adults don't have much income, they also don't have a ton of expenses and can usually knock off a good chunk of debt fairly quickly if they can maintain the discipline to do so. If she has really gotten into a mess, help her look into debt consolidation so she can make one payment instead of trying to keep track of several. These little steps won't make the debt go away, but they can make it more manageable.

Risk Taker

 Risk Takers won't be too bothered by debt. But they should be. Of all the Money Personalities, Risk Takers will be most in need of a balanced approach to debt.

The bottom line is that student loans and credit cards will be the tip of the debt iceberg if your Risk Taker isn't careful. This is the kid who is going to need loans to launch his abundant business ideas. He's going to borrow money to travel. He's going to want friends to invest in his ideas. If he's not paying attention, he can hit thirty years old owing a lot of money to a lot of people.

So talk with your Risk Taker early on about the importance of keeping his debt under control and paying off what he can, when he can. Encourage him to write up solid business plans for his big ideas so he can manage his resources well. And when you see him running too far or too quickly into a new adventure, check in with him about what it will mean for his overall debt picture. That voice of reason can help him avoid mountains of untamable debt.

Also, be clear with your Risk Taker about the dangers of shuffling money around. Risk Takers are prone to borrowing money from one source to pay off another source. Without someone warning them of the very real consequences of this practice, they can get caught up in a never-ending cycle of borrowing and paying, one that will make it nearly impossible for them to get ahead and truly live out the adventures they crave.

Security Seeker

If your Security Seeker has acquired some debt, fear not. All you need to say is, "How do you think this is going to factor into your future plans?" and she'll be off and running with a plan to pay off her debt in record time.

Security Seekers, like Savers, can be spooked by the idea of debt, so much so that they might miss out on opportunities that could be really good for them in the name of not taking on debt. So help your Security Seeker have the confidence in her own ability to plan and work with her resources to know that she can take a few chances now and then. Yes, a semester abroad might cost her a little more than a semester on campus, but what an incredible experience!

If your Security Seeker is already dealing with some debt, check in with her now and then to see how she's handling the payments. If she's struggling, she'll appreciate your help in sorting it out. If she's on schedule, she'll be thrilled to tell you how hard she has worked to pay it off. Either way, this conversation is a chance to strengthen your relationship with your Security Seeker.

Flyer

As with so many of these money conversations about dollars and accounts and payments, you'll need to tap into your Flyer's other Money Personality to help her figure out how to avoid and deal with debt.

Flyers won't always know they have debt. If they know, they won't really see it as a problem. That can work in their favor, because debt doesn't create a lot of stress for the Flyer. But if his Secondary Money Personality is a Saver or a Security Seeker, he might feel overwhelmed and uncertain about what to do with that debt. So use the skills inherent in that Money Personality and the ideas listed above to help him lay out a plan.

Button Pushers for Parents

Saver

Debt is a dirty word for Savers. Not only do they try to avoid it for themselves, but they have a tendency to judge others who carry a hefty debt too. That will go double for you if you see your child acquiring debt in her first few years out of the house.

So watch out for that tendency to be judgmental. You might be disappointed that your child doesn't have enough savings or that she seems to spend more than she earns. But shaming your child isn't going to make her debt go away. It's only going to make her pull away from you. Instead, talk through the reasons she has gotten into debt. You might find that it was somewhat unavoidable—she had to use her savings for car repairs and ended up needing a bigger student loan than she planned. Or she just hasn't gotten the hang of budgeting her own money yet and she could really use some help from you.

Work with your adult child in any way she wants you to—budgeting, checkbook balancing, working out a savings plan. And if she doesn't want your help, then keep the door open for further communication by showing her that you trust her to figure it out. And remember that unless she's a Saver, too, you're probably going to wish she was more conservative with her money. Do your best to let her make decisions based on her Money Personalities, not yours.

Spender

Spenders are fairly comfortable with debt, so you might find that you're not too concerned when your child has some. But we encourage you to talk about it anyway.

Debt can be a huge hindrance to young people. It can keep them from getting housing, transportation, small business loans, you name it. And since they typically don't have the means to reduce their debt quickly, it can keep them scrambling for years. So they need to take it seriously at this stage of life. You can help by talking openly about your own debt—where it came from, how you've dealt with it, what challenges it has presented. Even if you haven't been able to make much of a dent in your own debt, sharing your story can help your child see that it's something he needs to pay attention to and deal with as best he can.

Risk Taker

Oh, how Risk Takers love to leverage their assets! Debt is part of the game for Risk Takers, so they have a hard time understanding how anyone does anything *without* taking on some debt.

Your challenge will be to make sure you're not pressing

your adult child into taking financial risks she's not ready for or comfortable with. She might have a great business idea that you think she should work on now, but she wants to get a few years of real-world employment under her belt before she digs in. Let her move at her own pace, even if it means her big idea sits on the sidelines for a little while. Instead of resenting you for pushing her before she is ready, she'll be grateful for your trust in her instincts.

Security Seeker

We've heard so many Security Seekers express their fear that debt will ruin their future. They pass this same fear onto their adult children, cautioning them against any decision that might involve taking on debt.

It's essential to keep telling yourself—and your kids—that debt doesn't ruin anything. The way you handle that debt can make a huge difference in your future, but on its own, debt doesn't help or hurt you. It just is. So be careful not to turn debt into the boogeyman of finances. Some debt can be a necessary part of getting started on the road to financial security. If your adult child has accrued a good chunk of debt, offer your help in finding ways to reduce it—this is what you're best at, and you'll have invaluable ideas for making your child's debt a bit more manageable.

Flyer

These are tough conversations for Flyers, because there is a lot of potential conflict in talks about debt. If you're a Flyer and your adult child has built up a good chunk of debt, your instinct will be to say nothing for the sake of preserving the relationship. But that might not be the best idea.

If you're honest and straightforward with your child, this doesn't have to be a conflict-ridden conversation. Go ahead and admit that you're nervous about bringing up this topic because you don't ever want money to get in the way of your relationship. Then share your concerns about the damage that can come from mismanaged debt and your hopes that your child can find a way to bring that debt under control. If you have ideas for making that happen, don't hesitate to share them. Avoid judgment and blame and you're likely to make this a conversation that can draw you even closer to your child.

Lending Money

George is dreading this phone call. He knows it isn't going to go well, but he doesn't think he has any other options. He has messed up and needs help.

"Mom?"

"Hi, honey. How are you?"

"I'm okay, but I need a favor."

"What is it, sweetheart?"

"I need to borrow some money from you and Dad."

"Oh. How much were you thinking?"

"Well, I need about three thousand dollars, Mom."

The exasperated sigh and resulting silence on the other end tells George everything he needs to know. His parents will loan him the money, but there will be strings—so many strings—attached. He promised himself after the last time that he would never owe his parents money again, but this is unavoidable.

Last time, George had flown to Florida to visit a college friend. That trip had added about $1,000 to his already substantial credit card debt, so he asked his parents for a loan to reduce the debt by half. In return, he had to hand his credit card over to his parents for six months and pay back the loan with interest! He couldn't believe his own parents would charge him interest, but he was desperate. He was trying to rent an apartment and his lousy credit score was limiting his options. Getting that debt down did help him get into a place, so in the end, he figures it was worth it. But just barely.

This time the debt is really out of his control. His car has finally died, and he needs a vehicle to get to work. He has found a good car on Craigslist, but the seller wants cash or a certified check for the car, and George definitely doesn't have $2,500. He doesn't want to take out a loan from the bank—student loans and that credit card bill have him paying off too many people already. He would rather deal with his parents again than have to add another bank to his list of monthly payments.

He braces himself for the lecture that he knows is coming once his mother says yes to the loan. Yes, he should have done a better job saving money. Yes, he knows public transportation is an option. Yes, he should have learned his lesson by now. Yes, he knows he will have to pay his parents interest on the loan. Yes, he knows his dad isn't going to be happy about this.

After George thanks his mom and hangs up the phone, he wonders how he has gotten himself into this position again. He is twenty-four years old and has a pretty good job where he makes enough money to pay his rent and expenses. But it is never quite enough for him to have a cushion of any kind. So all it takes is one bad transmission and he is back to begging from his parents. He doesn't like it any more than they do, but he can't seem to figure out how to get ahead financially.

Remember that Fidelity study we mentioned in chapter 21? Of that $35,000 debt that awaits the average college graduate, $13,000 of it comes from personal and family loans. And those loans don't stop once a young adult gets out of school. For many young adults—those who go to college and those who don't—the parental purse strings are still their backup plan as they settle into apartments and jobs.

This is a tough position for parents. Whether or not you can afford to help your adult children with loans, you still need to determine if that's the best course of action. If you opt to loan your children money, you need to consider how they will pay you back or if you want them to pay you back (if you don't, make it clear this money is a gift, not a loan). If they pay you back, do they need to add interest? Will you set up a time limit? Is there a limit to the number of times they can borrow money from you?

The whole issue is fertile ground for money conflicts—between you and your child and between you and your parenting partner. That's why we highly suggest that parents put any agreements about loaning money to an adult child in writing. We call it a "Letter of Understanding," but you can call it whatever you like—just make sure you have something written down.

This letter doesn't have to be filled with legalese. It just needs to include the terms of the loan—how much money is being loaned, how long your child has to pay it back, how much, if any, interest she'll pay on the loan. We recommend having your child pay interest on any loan you give her, even if it's just 1 percent. This helps your child get used to the idea that when you borrow money, it costs you something. It's just one more little life lesson you can pass on to your child even while you're helping her out.

If borrowing money from you is starting to become a habit or a crutch that's keeping your child from learning how to live within her means, it might be time to say "no more" and cut off the money supply. That's not an easy conversation to have with your adult child. If you're so inclined, it can come with offers to help in other ways— working on a budget together, help with finding a second job or a cheaper housing situation—but be cautious of using money as a way of controlling or manipulating your child's behavior. A relationship based on what amounts to bribery—"We'll give you money if you come home more often"—isn't a healthy one. You'll be much better off as a family if you set clear expectations, avoid lectures, and let any loans remain business transactions, not signs of love or support.

While having a Letter of Understanding is a good general practice when you loan money to your child, it's not a substitute for good conversation about what the terms are of this loan. As you work through this conversation, make sure to address the specific issues unique to each Money Personality.

Here's how to talk about loaning money if your young adult child is a:

Saver

Your Saver isn't likely to ask for a loan, mostly because she will rarely need one. Savers know how to live well below their means, even to the point where they will deny themselves things they need, like new clothes or a more reliable car or a safer apartment to keep their budget in check. On those rare occasions when a Saver does ask for financial help, you can be sure she'll pay you back quickly, with interest. But just because she hardly ever asks for money doesn't mean you won't ever loan it to her.

The parents of Savers, especially those who aren't Savers themselves, will often see places where their adult child should be spending more but won't. The parents might go ahead and buy a better car for their child because they worry too much about that old clunker. They might outfit their child with new clothes to celebrate a new job. All of that is fine, as long as you are doing it out of love for your child and not the need to keep taking care of her. It might make you feel better, but it will make your Saver child feel worse.

Savers are very proud of the way they handle money. They pride themselves on getting by with less than other people. So if their parents jump in and try to provide for them, it doesn't go over as well as the parents might hope. Instead of seeing the gift for what it is, the Saver sees it as her parents wasting money on her or not trusting her ability to take care of herself. So despite all the good intentions you might have, talk to your Saver about these kinds of gifts before you give them. Ask if it's okay for you to celebrate her new job with a shopping spree or ease your own worries by pitching in on a better car. Let your Saver maintain control over her finances even as you try to help her out.

Spender

 If your Spender hasn't asked you for money already, it's only a matter of time. But before you get nervous about that, remember that just because Spenders love to spend doesn't mean they are irresponsible. If you lay out the terms of a loan clearly and keep track of your Spender's payments to you, there's no reason a loan can't be a great asset to your child.

The thing with Spenders is that they often don't have a lot of savings. So when they need a big chunk of money for a car or the down payment on a first home or a deposit on an apartment, they might not have it in hand. Those are the occasions when, if you're able, you can be a huge help to your adult child who is trying to get settled in his new life.

But if you find that your Spender is just not very good at keeping track of his money and seems to use you as his personal savings account, it might be time to set some limits on how much he can borrow and how often. If you are always the safety net, your Spender won't learn how to stand on his own two feet and make his own way. As hard as it can be to say no to your child, have an honest conversation about how he can deal with his money differently so that he's not dependent on you.

Risk Taker

Risk Takers and loans have a deep and lasting relationship. You've probably had plenty of experiences with your Risk Taker asking for some sort of loan. Even as young children, Risk Takers will talk their way into little loans from friends and family. That propensity for wheeling and dealing only intensifies as your child gets into adulthood, when she has real money and real opportunities for adventure and investments.

You'll need to establish some clear boundaries when it comes to loaning money to your Risk Taker. She will have no end to her big ideas and will always be looking for investors to fund her latest business venture or travel opportunity or educational endeavor. If you're not clear about how much and how often you're willing to be part of these plans, you could put your own financial stability at risk. There are plenty of places your Risk Taker can find funding for business ideas. You need to be her parents, not her venture capitalists.

That doesn't mean you need to say no to every request. It just means that you need to treat them as business decisions, not personal ones. If it seems like a good investment for you, then do it. But if you're handing over money only to make your Risk Taker happy, then take a step back and reevaluate.

Security Seeker

The Security Seeker is a great credit risk. While your Security Seeker will rarely ask for a loan—he has already planned for nearly every contingency—the reality is that even the best plans are no match for the ups and downs of life. So when your Security Seeker needs financial help from you, it will most likely be because his plans haven't worked the way he hoped they would.

Because of that, make sure to tread lightly on the emotional side of loaning money to your child. If you think you need to give him a good talking to about responsibility and planning ahead, save your breath. The Security Seeker already knows all of that and is likely feeling a good bit of shame in having to ask for help as it is. Instead of a lecture, lend a listening ear, a supportive shoulder, and if you want to and can afford to, a bit of money.

If you do lend money to your Security Seeker, have him help you work out the details of your agreement. He'll already have a strong sense of how much he can afford to pay you each month. And you can trust that if your Security Seeker makes a plan to pay you back, he'll follow through.

Flyer

 You might expect that you'll get lots of loan requests from your Flyer, but that's not necessarily the case. Since Flyers don't think about money very often, your Flyer is as likely to change plans in the face of financial need as she is to ask for help. If she needs first and last months' rent for an apartment, she might ask you for a loan, or she might just decide to find a different place to live.

If you loan money to your Flyer, however, be sure to have a clear, written agreement for how she'll repay the loan. And make sure she pays you on schedule. Your Flyer might forget to make a payment. She might skip a few and pay more another month. But keep on her and remind her that this agreement is all about mutual trust and respect, the hallmarks of a strong parent/adult child relationship.

Button Pushers for Parents

Saver

 The biggest challenge for a Saver parent who loans money to her kids won't just be keeping quiet about how her child could have avoided this need with more careful spending. It will be the loss of her own savings that gets to her.

Savers like to have cash on hand. It gives them a sense of safety and helps them feel in control of their finances. So when you loan money to your child, you are typically tapping into your own savings account. That can leave a Saver feeling anxious until the money is safely paid back and in the bank. Because of the stress this can create, we suggest Savers think long and hard before lending money to their children. Your relationship with your child is paramount. If lending money to him is going to leave you feeling edgy or checking up on how your adult child is spending "your" money, it's better for you to say no and protect your relationship.

Spender

 Spender parents are often quick to say yes to a loan request. It feels like one more way to use your money to bring joy to someone else. But it can create issues if you truly can't afford to make a loan.

Spenders chafe against feeling hemmed in on their money decisions. If lending money to your child means you have to reduce your own spending, it can lead you to resent your child for putting you in this spot. So say yes only if you can do so happily and with confidence that it won't have much impact on your financial situation.

Risk Taker

 As a Risk Taker, you've probably done plenty of asking for money yourself, so you likely feel fairly comfortable with this conversation in general. However, if you feel as though your child is using the money irresponsibly or to pay off debts she really should be able to handle on her own, you might start to get frustrated by the situation.

Risk Takers also need to make sure they are on the same page as their parenting partners on this one. If your child asks you to invest in her start-up company, every impulse in you is going to say yes! But hold back long enough to talk with your parenting partner about this decision. If you rush in on your own, you could be creating tension in your relationship with your parenting partner, something that won't help you or your adult child.

Security Seeker

 Security Seekers like being the ones making the plans. They get really uncomfortable being at the mercy of someone else's plans, especially if that someone else is their young adult child.

You'll find your buttons get pushed when your child is late on a payment or otherwise messes up your financial plans. If you're counting on that $200 repayment every month and it doesn't come, well, there go your books for the month. Even if you have plenty of room in your budget for a late payment, the fact that it's affecting your plans will ruin your Security Seeker mojo. So make sure you are helping your child stay on top of the payments. When he's not, talk calmly with him about the impact that has on your budget. Help him understand that there's another budget at play here besides his.

Flyer

 Flyers need to think long and hard about lending money to their adult children. So much of what you value in your relationship with your child—communication, trust, honesty—can be put in jeopardy if the loan arrangement goes bad. We've seen adult children default on loans from their parents and just stop talking to them for a while, because they can't face the conversation. We've seen Flyer parents start to resent the way their adult children come to them when they want money, then never call or visit. Because relationships are far more important than money to a Flyer, the risks they take here have nothing to do with budgets or cash or repayments. They have everything to do with the relationship.

Before you say yes to a loan, talk with your child about what might go wrong and how you will deal with it together. You need to make sure you have a written Letter of Understanding for your child's sake as well as your own so you aren't tempted to just let your agreement slide in order to keep the peace with your child. Talk about all the possibilities. What should she do if she misses a payment? What if she needs more money than she thought? What are other situations that might come up where she could need a loan, and what other options does she have? Get everything on the table and move ahead cautiously.

23

Moving Home

Ruby has been out of college for almost a year. She graduated with a degree in sociology and has plans to go to graduate school soon. Really soon. But she worked so hard her last year of school that she is pretty burned out, so she decides to take a year off from studying and get a job. She moves to a large city about an hour from where she grew up and gets an apartment with a high school friend. Ruby pieces together some jobs—assistant manager at a retail store, a good waitressing job at a chain restaurant—and she is doing fine. But now her roommate is getting married, and Ruby has a decision to make—stay put or move on.

While this last year has been fun—no stress, a little disposable income, lots of free time on the weekends—Ruby is struggling with what to do next. So many of her friends are beginning their careers or getting married or buying houses or going on to graduate school that she's starting to feel like a loser for wasting her education on a retail job. She keeps telling people this is all temporary and that she's going to grad school, but she hasn't taken any steps to make that happen.

Now that her roommate is leaving, she wonders if it's worth the hassle of finding a new roomie or if she should just pack up, move back to her parents' house, and get serious about either applying for grad programs or applying for jobs in her field. The more she weighs her options, the better it sounds to be back in her old room, not worrying about rent or groceries, and focusing her energy on getting into school.

Ruby's parents, of course, don't quite see it that way. When Ruby tosses the idea out during a phone call, Ruby's mother is at a loss. She doesn't want to say no—it is Ruby's home after all, and of course she's always welcome there. But her mom doesn't want to coddle Ruby. Ruby's parents have seen her mature a lot in the last year. Having to find her own housing and get jobs has been a good experience for Ruby, and they want to see her keep moving forward, not backward. They worry that if they let her move back home, she won't have the motivation she needs to pursue grad school or a more professional career path.

Today's young adults are being called the *boomerang generation* because they keep coming back home! It's not unusual for a recent college grad to spend at least a summer at home, if not several months. And it's becoming increasingly common for adult children who are well past college to move back in with their parents when a job falls through or a marriage ends or they are transitioning from one stage to another.

This puts parents in a strange bind. While we always

want our children to feel loved and welcomed in their childhood homes, we also don't want them to get so comfortable there that they get stuck. And that's on top of the many money decisions that come along with letting adult children move home. Will you make her pay some rent? Does she need to buy her own groceries? Can she use the family car? All of these questions need to be dealt with *before* a child moves back in.

Ruby's parents also need to make sure they are on the same page before they give Ruby the go-ahead. If one parent is all for it and the other thinks it's a terrible idea, there will be tremendous tension in the family. They also need to make sure they can afford having another person in the house. Even if Ruby pays some rent or contributes to the meals, having another person around the house adds to the expenses.

Still, having Ruby live at home for a time could be a great move for all of them. This unexpected time together gives Ruby's parents the opportunity to offer her a bit more guidance as she thinks more seriously about her future. She might benefit from having her parents around to bounce ideas off of or to be her moral support as she faces potential rejection from schools or employers. They can help her build even better money management skills as she figures out how to pay for grad school. And without the busyness that comes from having two jobs, Ruby will have more time to commit to getting her plans together.

If your adult child is considering moving back in with you for a month or more, you'll need to have some intentional conversations about how this arrangement will work.

Having all the expectations out on the table will greatly reduce the potential for tension and conflict. As you talk through the details, keep your child's Money Personalities in mind.

Here's how to talk about moving back home if your child is a:

Saver

 Of all the Money Personalities, the Saver might be the most inclined to move back in with Mom and Dad. What better way is there to reduce expenses than to live rent free? If you get the feeling your Saver is considering moving in with you just to save money, it's time to take a firm stance with him.

Start by talking about the importance of learning how to save money while still covering his own expenses. This is one of those major life skills that, while fairly obvious to most people, won't really occur to your young adult. He's going to see the no-brainer option—living with you—in front of him and stop thinking about alternative plans. So before you say yes to a new tenant, make sure he has actually exhausted his other options. If he truly can't find an affordable place to live or he's waiting on a job offer before he settles somewhere, put an end date on his "lease." He can stay for three months or two weeks or whatever seems reasonable.

You can also use this time to help your Saver get a sense of what it really costs to live in the real world. If your Saver hasn't lived on his own yet, have him sit down with you as you make your budget each month. Take him to the grocery store with you and have him compare prices for the food he likes to eat. Have him help you write out your utility payments. He needs to see that there is more to living with you than having a bed to sleep in. He needs to know just how much you are really saving him so that when he does venture out on his own, he knows what to expect. With his skills at saving money, he'll have no trouble making it all work out, but only when he's aware of just what it costs to cover his basic needs.

Spender

 If your Spender wants to move home, look out! A Spender with little to no living expenses and a source of income is going to blow every penny she makes. And that's not really the reason you're letting her live at home. So before your Spender sets her suitcase on the floor of your house, you'll need to have an honest conversation with her about expectations—yours and hers.

Start by having her think about what she wants to accomplish in her time at home. Is it a chance to save some money? Is it buying her time to think through her next move? Is it a layover between college and grad school? A stopping place while she plans her wedding? Whatever it is, she needs to have a clear goal for her time with you. If she's just looking for a free place to stay so she can live it up, you won't be doing her any favors by letting her crash with you indefinitely.

Once she has set a goal, do what you can to help her reach it, knowing that some goals will require more guidance from you than others. If she's trying to save some money, remember that it's not in her Spender nature to do so, and help her stick with some kind of spending budget each week. You could even have her pay you a bit of rent, set it aside if you can, then give that money back to her when she leaves to use as a deposit on an apartment. If her goals involve finding a job or applying to graduate programs, check in with her now and then to see how she's doing. Try not to nag or cajole her, but gently remind her that her stay has an endpoint.

Risk Taker

 Your Risk Taker is unlikely to move home because he can't find anywhere to live. A Risk Taker can always figure out a living situation, because nothing is too out-there for him. Move in with eight friends and four dogs? No problem. Live out of a van for three months while he and his buddies tour the West Coast? Why not? No, the Risk Taker will most likely want to move in with you because his Plan A (and B and C and D) have fallen through and he needs a place to regroup.

You might find, then, that your Risk Taker is fairly vulnerable when he asks to move in with you. Something he was excited about has gone off the rails, and now he has to refocus and figure out what his next adventure will be. You can help him through this process by assisting him to see that the mere act of moving into independence and adulthood is an adventure in itself.

When your Risk Taker was younger, his risk-taking behavior was mingled with his developing brain. But as he gets older, he will start to see that adventure doesn't have to involve a great wave or a big idea. Sometimes it can be finding a steady job that has a level of risk in it. It can be taking a chance on a solid relationship. It can be the occasional awesome trip to some interesting place instead of a constant search for the best and the wildest. Help him ease into this more mature understanding of life and you'll see him get his feet under him and move forward in no time.

You will also need to decide if you are willing to help fund his next big adventure. Risk Takers have no problem risking their own money, and they are pretty comfortable talking their friends and family into those risks too. If your child is trying to move forward with an idea and wants your financial help, make sure you can afford the risk before you say yes.

Security Seeker

 Security Seekers can be a bit of a mystery in this area. Since they are terrific planners, it's unlikely they will want to move in and stay indefinitely—they will have a plan for moving on. At the same time, the idea of living at home and being able to check "housing" off the list of money decisions is tempting for any young adult, but especially Security Seekers. So you'll need to keep communicating with your

Security Seeker about any potential move before and during his stay so you have a good sense of what he needs and why he needs it.

If your Security Seeker asks to move home, make the most of his planning abilities and have him lay out exactly how this will work before you agree. What will he pay for? How long does he intend to stay? If you have thoughts about those things, this is the time to bring them up. Your Security Seeker needs to know what you expect. When he does, he will work out his plans to make sure everyone gets what they want out of this arrangement.

Flyer

 This is not going to be a one-time conversation with your Flyer. Because your Flyer has likely based most of her life decisions so far on everything but financial considerations, she might find herself in her early or midtwenties without much money or savings or ideas about what she wants to do next. So she might very well pop in and out of your house more than once in her young adult years.

But that doesn't mean she's incapable of making solid plans. She just needs your help to get them moving. When and if your Flyer child lives with you for a bit, use that time to check in on her money situation. What kind of savings does she have? How realistic are her plans for work or housing or travel? Remember, these are issues Flyers truly don't think about, and they need guidance to put financial plans together.

You'll also need to make sure you lay out very clear expectations for how this living arrangement will work. Your Flyer won't think about the fact that someone pays for the food that magically appears in the fridge or that it costs money to keep that hot water flowing. Again, she's not dumb; she just doesn't think about money—ever. So if you want her to pay a bit of rent and contribute to the groceries and utilities, you'll need to lay that out ahead of time. And be sure to agree to an end point for this arrangement. Your Flyer needs to know the day is coming when she'll have to support herself.

Button Pushers for Parents

If you and your parenting partner decide to let one of your adult children live with you for a time, be ready for plenty of potential conflict. If you know your Money Personality hot buttons, you'll be better prepared to ward off those conflicts and replace them with good communication and clear expectations.

Saver

 When your adult child asks to move back home, the first thing you'll see will be dollar signs. But you won't just have your own finances on your mind; you'll be thinking about your child's as well. You might find yourself frustrated that your child hasn't saved enough to afford to live on her own or that she's having a hard time making ends meet. And while those things might be true, you'll need to keep your frustration to yourself.

Instead, channel it into constructive help for your young adult. If she's not great at saving money, use this time to help her develop a few skills. Unless she's a Saver, too, she probably won't have the same standard of how much she should save as you do, so work with real numbers—how much will she actually need for an apartment or grad school or travel, and how can she work on saving up for it? Be patient, be encouraging, and be ready to keep having these conversations during her stay.

Spender

Spenders can be surprisingly testy when they feel they're being used. And if ever there was a situation ripe for feeling used, it's having your adult child move back home. Your instinct will be to say yes and not expect your child to pay anything. But we suggest putting a few money plans in place to help you avoid being seen as a rent-free crash pad.

You might be content to foot the bill for your adult child while he's at home, but it will be a bigger benefit to him and to your relationship if you have him contribute something. This prepares him for life on his own and prevents you from feeling like you're being taken advantage of, both of which will pay off when your child finally heads out on his own.

Risk Taker

For the Risk Taker parent, an adult child coming back to the nest is less about the money decisions that come into play and more about the disappointment that this child needs to come home at all. Risk Takers have huge dreams for their kids, and it can be hard to watch them struggle to move forward.

Risk Takers need to take care, then, to not pass on that disappointment to their kids. If your adult child wants to move back home for a bit, remember that jumping into adult life is harder now than it was even a generation ago. It's not a sign of failure to have a hard time finding a good job or an affordable place to live. It's not the end of the dream just because it's taking a little longer than you had hoped.

Security Seeker

 Your biggest frustration is likely to be that your adult child is both interrupting your plans and not following through on his own. Security Seekers have the future all mapped out, including how they will spend both the time and money that get freed up when kids leave home. So when one of those kids comes back, the plan is thrown off course. And that makes Security Seekers nervous.

You might also find yourself irritated with an adult child who doesn't seem to have much of a plan other than living in your basement for what can seem like an eternity. Rather than assume he has nothing better to do than watch your TV, keep talking to your young adult and find out what plans he does have. There might not be much there, but try to work with what is there—hopes for grad school, an internship opportunity, a job offer. Then use what you know about making plans to help your young adult follow up on his leads. As you do, you might find that he has more going on than you thought, something that will help ease everyone's nerves.

Flyer

Flyer parents are going to jump on the idea of having their kids move back home. It sounds so great in theory. But in practice, even Flyer parents can get broadsided by the tensions that can come from having an adult child living at home. You might go into this thinking it's going to be a big lovefest, only to find that your adult child basically sleeps at your house and then disappears all day. Instead of a closer relationship, you have a renter who never comes to dinner.

To avoid feeling used or rejected, Flyer parents need to set out clear expectations for their adult children living at home. If you want your child to have dinner with you once a week, tell him. If it's important to you that he help out with your younger kids or pitch in on household tasks, tell him. Be honest and up front about what you want so you and your child can keep your relationship strong and healthy.

24

Money Personality Goals for Ages 18 and Beyond

ike nearly everything else in this launching stage of your child's life, it's now time to hand over the goal setting to your adult child. So instead of helping you set action-oriented goals with your young adult, we're going to focus on conversations that can help expand your child's Money Personalities and strengthen your Money Relationship.

This is also the time to start telling your own stories about money decisions you've made in your life. Talk to your young adult about both the good financial choices you've made and the mistakes you regret. The point isn't to get your child to copy everything you did right and avoid everything you did wrong. It's to make your Money Relationship even stronger by opening up honest conversations about money decisions so your young adult can see that when it comes to money, everyone has strengths and everyone has challenges.

Goals for Savers

Start with some encouragement for your young adult's Money Personalities. Give examples of times you've seen your Saver make tough choices in order to get a good deal or save money.

Then get him talking about spending. Ask something like: If all of your bills were paid and you had $100 to spend any way you like, what would bring you joy? If you had to give it away, to whom would you give it?

Talk about risk taking: Who do you know that has been a Risk Taker in life? What admirable things have you seen that person accomplish? What risks have you taken that you're proud of?

Talk about relationships: How do you see money helping your relationships? Do you ever see money hurting relationships?

These conversations can spark ideas in your Saver for being more generous, more adventuresome, and more relationship-oriented.

Goals for Spenders

Praise your Spender's generosity. Talk about times when you've seen him give away his own resources to help someone else.

Then talk about saving: Have you ever had

a time when you wanted to give something to a friend and you couldn't because you didn't have the money? What would it mean for you to have some money saved up to use in those situations? What would you want to change in your spending habits?

Talk about risk and security for the future: What do you think your first apartment or house will be like? What adventures do you see yourself having in the next five years? If you could guarantee one aspect of your future, what would it be?

These conversations can help your Spender think about ways to plan for the future and balance her spending with savings that can make those plans a reality.

Goals for Risk Takers

 Encourage your Risk Taker's adventuresome spirit. Offer some examples of times when you've admired his ability to take a risk.

Then talk about savings: What adventures seem out of reach because of finances? What kind of business would you start if someone gave you $5,000? How long do you think it would take you to save $5,000?

Talk about planning for the future: You love to think about your next adventure. What other plans do you have for the next few years? What would it feel like for you to know that you have money set aside for future experiences? What sacrifices would you have to make now? Would it be worth it?

These conversations can help your Risk Taker start

thinking of ways to balance spending and savings to fund his own great adventures.

Goals for Security Seekers

Compliment your Security Seeker on her planning skills. Tell her about times in her life when you've noticed her making plans and working toward them.

Then talk about spending: What have you spent your money on that has brought you joy? When does spending money feel scary to you? Think of someone you know whose future isn't secure. How could you use your resources to help that person?

Talk about taking risks: What's the most interesting thing you've done in the last year? What's one exciting thing you want to do in the next year? Tell me about a risk you've taken recently.

Talk about relationships: What ideas do you have for taking care of your family one day? What makes you feel secure in a relationship?

These questions can inspire your Security Seeker to be less anxious about the future and consider ways to enjoy the here and now.

Goals for Flyers

Praise your Flyer for his focus on relationships. Tell him about a time when you've been impressed by the way he cares for other people.

Then talk about spending and saving: If you were able to take a trip anywhere in the world, where would you go? Whom would you take with you? What would it take for you to really do something like that?

Talk about the future: Where do you see yourself living in a year? In five years? In ten? Does thinking about the future make you nervous or excited? How can you make sure it's a little of both?

Conversations like these can help your Flyer start thinking about the ways good money decisions can strengthen her relationships.

Make It Happen!

25

Making It Happen!

Like so much in parenthood, helping your children build strong, healthy money habits takes patience, time, and lots of repetition. We expect that you'll revisit the conversations in this book more than once as your children grow and change. But we're confident that as you do, you'll see them learning to talk about and deal with money in ways that make the most of their Money Personalities.

We also know that the more you see your kids' Money Personalities at work, the more you're going to notice your own Money Personalities playing into these conversations and the money decisions you make as a family. And we hope you'll see that as a starting point for a whole family money makeover. As we've learned more about our individual Money Personalities and our sons' Money Personalities, we've found ourselves seriously rethinking the way we make money decisions as a couple and as a family. It's as if we've cracked a mystery code and found an amazing treasure as a result.

That treasure is a reasonably harmonious family life.

Of course we still argue about silly things like every other family on the planet. And we still have money problems that need solving. But here's what has happened: We don't have big, dramatic, drawn-out battles over money—not as a couple and not as parents. When we do disagree about a money decision—and we do—we don't get worked up about it because we know it's a hurdle we can clear with some calm conversation and mutual respect for the other person's Money Personalities. Since nearly every part of life involves a money component, having the language and skills to navigate that piece of our day-to-day lives means there is less tension in our family, less stuff to argue about.

We have a saying that you've probably noticed throughout this book: Make It Happen! This has been our mantra for the last three years as we've encouraged couples—and now parents—to change the way they think about and talk about money. We chose these words for a reason. Good money habits don't just fall into place. Kids don't just know how to save or give or spend wisely. A lot of adults don't know how to do those things either! But when we get intentional about learning new ways to communicate, when we put in the time and effort to discover and respect our Money Personalities and those of the people we love, we can make real change happen.

We've seen couples come back from the brink of divorce because they made it happen. We've seen families that were falling apart over money issues work together and recover because they made it happen. And we've seen parents put an end to the begging, whining, and other battles that come when kids lack money skills because they made it happen.

Whether your child is five or twenty-five, you can make it happen too.

So when we encourage you to have these money conversations with your kids, it's not just because we want to help you develop good money habits in your children. It's because we believe that when families know how to talk about money, when they understand the Money Personalities at play in their relationships, they really are happier. Now it's your turn. Make It Happen!

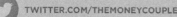

The 5 money conversations to have

31290096091699 CA